THE PLAYFUL WAY

CREATIVITY, CONNECTION, AND JOY THROUGH EVERYDAY MOMENTS OF PLAY

THE PLAYFUL WAY

PIERA GELARDI

HarperOne

An Imprint of HarperCollinsPublishers

Without limiting the exclusive rights of any author, contributor or the publisher of this publication, any unauthorized use of this publication to train generative artificial intelligence (AI) technologies is expressly prohibited. HarperCollins also exercise their rights under Article 4(3) of the Digital Single Market Directive 2019/790 and expressly reserve this publication from the text and data mining exception.

THE PLAYFUL WAY. Copyright © 2026 by Piera Gelardi. All rights reserved. No part of this book may be used or reproduced in any manner whatsoever without written permission except in the case of brief quotations embodied in critical articles and reviews. For information, address HarperCollins Publishers, 195 Broadway, New York, NY 10007. In Europe, HarperCollins Publishers, Macken House, 39/40 Mayor Street Upper, Dublin 1, D01 C9W8, Ireland.

HarperCollins books may be purchased for educational, business, or sales promotional use. For information, please email the Special Markets Department at SPsales@harpercollins.com.

hc.com

FIRST EDITION

Designed by Bonni Leon-Berman
Art © Sensvector/Shutterstock

Library of Congress Cataloging-in-Publication Data has been applied for.

ISBN 978-0-06-341669-7

Printed in the United States of America

26 27 28 29 30 LBC 5 4 3 2 1

To my family
for teaching me to see the tiny lampshade
in every toothpaste cap, the Gumby bend
in every rule, and the pink flamingos
hiding in plain sight all over Brooklyn

And to
the wild, playful spirit that lives in each of
us, ready to shake loose and run free

PLAYFUL
curiously,
creatively,
courageously
engaged
with life

When we're in a state of play
Our truest selves come out to say:
"I'm here! Alive! Awake right now!"
Busy thoughts can say ciao, ciao
Dancing with life, in full delight
No script, no rehearsal, no need to be "right"
Just curious, wild, connected, and free
Play is where we remember to be

CONTENTS

Introduction		1
Chapter 1	Unzip Your Serious Suit	25
	Your "Unzip Your Serious Suit" Toolkit	40
Chapter 2	Look for Pink Flamingos	43
	Your "Looking for Pink Flamingos" Toolkit	54
Chapter 3	Practice the Playful Way	57
	Your "Practice the Playful Way" Toolkit	73
Chapter 4	Strike Gold in Boredom	77
	Your "Strike Gold in Boredom" Toolkit	88
Chapter 5	Play with Shadows	91
	Your "Play with Shadows" Toolkit	105
Chapter 6	Move Out of Your Head	109
	Your "Move Out of Your Head" Toolkit	125
Chapter 7	Renew Your Wows	129
	Your "Renew Your Wows" Toolkit	140
Chapter 8	Try It and See	143
	Your "Try It and See" Toolkit	154
Chapter 9	Don't Eat Yourself Alive!	157
	Your "Don't Eat Yourself Alive!" Toolkit	170
Conclusion	The World Awaits Your Playful Spirit	173
Acknowledgments		179
Bibliography		183

THE PLAYFUL WAY

INTRODUCTION

CALLING YOU BACK TO THE PLAYGROUND

The airport is chaos. Lines snake beyond the designated barriers and out the doors as frazzled travelers tug their luggage and scowl at their phones, their grimacing faces even more dramatic in the harsh lighting.

I stand in the security queue, sensing the stress emanating from everyone around me like swarms of buzzing flies. A man behind me huffs with dramatic indignation, a couple ahead bickers in hissed whispers—"We should have left earlier!"—and someone's roller bag keeps thwacking my heels.

My fists clench as irritation winds me tighter. The security checkpoint seems miles away and my flight is in an hour. I feel myself being sucked into the collective vortex of misery.

Then, as we make our first zig in the queue, I catch my partner's eye and make a split-second decision. I raise my hand for a high five.

"Yes!" I exclaim with exaggerated enthusiasm. "One turn closer!"

My partner looks momentarily confused, then a half grin lights up his face as he slaps my raised palm. A spark of mischief passes through us. A few people nearby glance over, some with bemused smiles.

When we reach the next turn, we're ready. "Turn number TWO!" we announce together, high-fiving with gusto. A woman behind us lets out a chuckle that seems to surprise even herself.

By the third turn, a family with a toddler holds up their hands for high fives before we can even offer ours. "We're on a roll now!" the dad says, grinning.

With each zigzag, our celebration grows a little as others join our absurd incremental progress party. Soon, a pocket of genuine laughter has formed in our section of the line, spreading outward like ripples from a skipped rock as others catch on to our game.

In that moment of travel chaos, we made a choice: Instead of facing the frustrating situation with tense resentment (what I call "the Pressured Way"), we transformed it with levity ("the Playful Way"). This simple shift didn't change our situation—we were still in the same painfully slow airport security queue, still at risk of missing our flight. But it changed what it felt like—shifting stress into humor, isolation into community.

The choice between the Pressured Way and the Playful Way appears constantly in our lives: during technology crashes, tricky conversations, power struggles, and canceled plans. When challenges arise, we can clench our jaws and white-knuckle our way through, or we can bring imagination, inquiry, and openness to the situation.

This choice isn't just about boosting fun (though that's a welcome bonus), it's about accessing new solutions, deeper camaraderie, and a richer experience of everyday life.

While our airport moment involved a social game, your playful response might look different: finding beauty in the terminal architecture, cracking a joke with your travel mate, or putting on music and imagining the scene as a film. Whatever form it takes, playfulness means approaching the situation with curious creativity: treating it as raw material for possibility, not just an obstacle to endure.

THE SCIENCE OF ADULT PLAYFULNESS

Playfulness is often dismissed as frivolous—a charming but dispensable quality best left in childhood alongside stuffies and imaginary friends.

But watch any child transform a cardboard box into a spaceship or a pile of sticks into a fairy house, and (beyond the cute façade) you are witnessing them exercising some of humanity's most valuable abilities: imagination, adaptation, and ingenuity.

Somewhere along the way to adulthood, many of us tucked these qualities into storage. We were taught that success comes through seriousness, that productivity trumps play, that "growing up" means leaving playfulness behind.

But what if that conventional wisdom is entirely backward?

Research reveals that playful adults excel at problem-solving and stress management and consistently report higher life satisfaction (Proyer 2013). They're keen observers who spot fresh perspectives where others see only obstacles. They develop healthier coping mechanisms and bounce back faster from setbacks too. As Dr. Stuart Brown from the National Institute for Play puts it, "The opposite of play is not work. It's depression."

Playfulness is an underestimated trait that's more Swiss Army knife than cheap toy. It's an incredibly handy tool for handling life's complexities. It's got corkscrews for opening up possibilities, scissors for cutting through perfectionism, a magnifying glass for finding solutions, and tweezers for extracting joy from the teensy-tiniest of spaces.

Beyond the mental, playfulness also benefits our bodies. Studies link it to lower stress, improved immune function, better cognitive function, and even longer lives. Playfulness isn't just a nice-to-have; it's essential for anyone who wants to live a healthier, happier life.

Despite these benefits, we're facing what researchers call "play deprivation" (yes, that's an actual scientific term!). This comes with real costs: it contributes to increased anxiety, pessimism, diminished creativity, and difficulty adapting to change.

I've noticed these effects in my own life and in the lives of those around me: The high-achieving exec who forgot how to celebrate her successes and now feels like a ghost in her own life. The parent who turned into a drill sergeant at home, wishing they could just be silly again. The creative team frozen in fear, unable to unleash their imaginations. The midcareer professional who draws a blank when asked what brings them joy, having been so busy being responsible that they've lost track of what lights them up. The recent graduate who's terrified to try different paths because they might pick the "wrong" one.

The good news? Playfulness is part of us all. It's standard issue for the human species. Even if you've left yours in the drawer gathering dust, you can pick it up again. This book is your user manual to guide you, regardless of your starting point.

If you're already a play enthusiast, *The Playful Way* will give you reason to go deeper, map uncharted territories, and spread your playful light to others.

A PLAYFUL MINDSET

When I talk about playfulness in adulthood, I'm often met with puzzled looks. "You mean sports?" people ask. Or "Board games?" "Oh, like, work hard / play hard . . . partying?"

But playfulness runs deeper than scheduled recreation (though that is important). It's not a leisure activity reserved for weekends or vacations. It's a mindset that transforms how we experience everything.

Playfulness is:

- Finding humor and lightness even in tense moments
- Staying open to possibilities rather than fixating on one "right" way
- Experimenting rather than seeking perfection
- Bringing an ethos of curious exploration to difficulties
- Finding wisdom in the body when the mind's tied up in knots
- Tuning your attention to notice details and find wonder
- Reimagining dull tasks through reframes and games
- Improvising when things go sideways

When we move through the world playfully, we stay loose and nimble. We adapt faster, roll with changes, collaborate with challenges, and transform tedious tasks into little adventures.

MY PLAYFUL PATH

Playfulness has been my compass through life's twists and turns, helping me navigate everything from career transitions and fertility struggles to depression and anxiety. When conventional wisdom falls short, play shows me the way forward.

This approach to life was born in the kitchen of my childhood home, with its cheerful painted tiles, bright green countertops, and wall jam-packed with family photos. After my brother and I helped our parents serve dinner, the fun began. My words would tumble out in excitement: "Hey, what if we started a kids' karaoke club?" My parents would exchange a conspiratorial glance. "Now, there's an idea!" Mom would reply, leaning forward. "What would that look like? Where would we host it?"

Between bites of penne, my brother would chime in: "We could have themed nights: Disney songs one week, pop hits the next!" My dad would smile, his laughter-creased eyes twinkling. "I love it! Now, what would we name it?" Before anyone could answer, his fork was in the air, face lit up with enthusiasm. "Ooh! Ooh! Ooh! I know! Kiddieoke!"

These kitchen table sessions were boisterously loud as we built upon each other's ideas. No idea was too outrageous to explore. We were elementary schoolers doing business brainstorms and our parents took us seriously and egged us on.

Eventually, we'd have to clear the table, do our homework, and return to our daily responsibilities. But in these moments, I learned that any endeavor could be handled with an inquisitive attitude and a willingness to explore.

I was fortunate to have parents who showed me that wonder and whimsy could be woven into all aspects of life. My mom (a social worker, artist, gardener) and my dad (an entrepreneur, engineer, inventor) modeled what it looks like for adults to be playful while simultaneously building businesses, dealing with illness and loss, and nurturing families and communities.

This spirit of adventure carried me to New York City, where I co-founded and built Refinery29 from a small style website into one of the most influential digital media brands for women, reaching millions with its distinctive mix of fashion, culture, and boundary-pushing storytelling.

Even in the workplace, I carved out spaces for play, like my apricot-colored office (dubbed "the Peach Pit") with its round table that became our magic circle for brainstorms. All the players around the table now were adults, so I had to take some extra measures to get the ideas flowing, like doing physical shake breaks and buzzing a lovingly bedazzled Taboo game buzzer when anyone got into an excessively serious "idea killer" mode.

Our playful approach led us to create innovative experiences like 29Rooms—a funhouse that reimagined vacant warehouses into kaleidoscopic, artist-made wonderlands where a hundred thousand adults came through to frolic and fall down imagination rabbit holes.

In 2021, I began a new chapter after leaving the company I'd built over fifteen years. But the transition was like moving out of a home you've loved—even when you're ready to go, there's still a bittersweet ache. Add to that the wild adventure of new motherhood and a global pandemic, and I was navigating multiple identity shifts at once. Daunting questions loomed: Who was I beyond the role I was most known for? What kind of parent would I become? What did I want to create next?

As I faced these huge transitions, my spirit whispered an answer: experiment! Instead of rushing to figure it all out, I turned my life into a play laboratory. I led cathartic dance parties on Zoom, created public art experiences connecting strangers in parks, took classes in improv and storytelling, and said yes to pretty much any foray that sparked curiosity. I dove deep into researching the power of play for our health and happiness, and piles of books stacked up on my desk.

As my calendar filled up with what I lovingly called "play dates with possibility" and I led thousands of people in creative exploration, I discovered my next chapter—making spaces for playful, creative practice and shared joy.

Playfulness has been my life preserver across all aspects of my life. As a teenager exploring my queerness, it let me move forward with joyful curiosity rather than fear. As an adult living with depression and anxiety, it nudged me to find movement when my mind wouldn't budge. When my neurodivergent brain has needed extra support, it helped me work with my rhythms instead of fighting them. My relationship with playfulness has kept me afloat and splashing around.

I've developed my own tricks and tools for sparking playfulness and seen the power of this approach transform not just my own life but those of many others I've worked with. And now I'm on a mission to unlock that magic for you too—to help you dive into that giddy river that flows when we approach life with playfulness.

YOUR PLAYBOOK

This book is a practical guide to living with more creativity, connection, and joy. Each chapter has stories from real people, research-backed insights, and play practices you can try today. Through perspective shifts and playful experiments, you'll learn to:

- Dance around the voices that say play is frivolous (I call them the Anti-Play Posse)
- Figure out which of the eight Powers of Play you are
- Transform both ordinary moments and major obstacles
- Navigate life's uncertainties with more grace and less anxiety
- Build spaces where imagination can breathe
- Find kinship, collaboration, and camaraderie with those around you

My hope is that *The Playful Way* becomes your trusted companion: a permission slip and road map to creating a life that feels less like a series of problems to solve and more like an adventure.

Our world desperately needs more playfulness, more creative solutions, more authentic connections, more joy. It needs more of us to choose the Playful Way. It needs YOU to return to the playground.

Will you come play with me?

If you are curious,
no answer is final.

If you live in wonder,
you can find joy.

If you practice seeing
possibility, there is hope.

If you learn to improvise,
you find solutions on the fly.

If you can bend, you will not break.

If you are playful, you are
creatively connected to life.

REKINDLE THINGS WITH YOUR OLD FRIEND PLAY

YOUR PLAYFUL SPIRIT HAS BEEN WAITING FOR YOUR PHONE CALL

Internal Grumbling

As we head toward playland, there might be some internal grumbling that needs to be addressed head-on. On the path to adulthood, playfulness gets a bad rap as unproductive, a silly distraction from the "serious business" of growing up.

This happens for all kinds of reasons. Some are structural and painful—adverse childhood experiences that force us to grow up too quickly or systemic inequalities that make playfulness unsafe or inaccessible. The playground isn't equally open to everyone, and some of us had to become vigilant adults long before our time.

Even for those with smoother paths, our schools and workplaces whisper (and sometimes shout) that success comes from seriousness. Capitalism hits us with constant messages that our worth comes from what we produce or what we own, not from how vividly alive and ourselves we are.

Whatever the cause, the pattern forms: We trade curiosity for certainty, exploration for efficiency, and spontaneity for strategic planning. We pack away presence in pursuit of future goals. We forget how to play because we're so busy learning how to work.

And let's be honest. Being playful requires a vulnerability that isn't always accessible or safe in every situation. Consider these common scenarios:

"I'd love to share this playful idea in the meeting, but as the only woman of color on the team, I worry about being taken seriously."

"In professional settings, I tone down my naturally animated self. As someone with ADHD, my spontaneous wordplay and creative tangents are how my brain naturally works, but I've learned to mask these to appear more 'focused' and 'professional.'"

"As someone who grew up working class and made it to the executive level, I worry that being playful will make people remember I don't "belong" here. Even though I have creative ideas for team building, I stick to traditional approaches because I'm already working twice as hard to be taken seriously."

"At family gatherings, I carefully filter my stories and enthusiasm. As a queer person who's not out to my extended family, playfulness feels risky—what if I accidentally reveal too much of myself?"

These concerns are totally valid. The goal isn't to be playful everywhere all at once, but to nurture play where it feels safe, gradually expanding those spaces while honoring our need for security. Sometimes being playful might look like small private moments: a little dance around the kitchen when no one's watching, or a creative daydream during your commute. Other times it might mean finding communities where your authentic playful self is celebrated.

And remember: if you're in a position of power, taking the risk to be playful can be a huge permission slip for those around you to do the same.

Now let's learn how to speak back to some of the voices that tell us not to play.

Quiet the Anti-Play Posse

One of the biggest barriers to being playful (or doing anything else courageous) is those voices in our heads that tell us not to. They screech: "You'll embarrass yourself!" "This is stupid." "You have a reputation to protect."

How did those voices get there? Well, likely they're the echoes of parents, teachers, bosses, or other authority figures that stomped on our playful spirits at some point in time. Or they could be the product of societal expectations we've internalized.

Recognizing and naming the anti-play voices can lessen their power to stop us from being our authentically playful selves. I'm calling these bullies the Anti-Play Posse, and here's how we'll stand up to them confidently and with compassion.

The Workaholic: "You're wasting your time with play. Success is all about hard work, discipline, and productivity. Be efficient."
Your Response: "I know you feel pressure, but burning out won't make me more successful. Research shows that play breaks improve focus and problem-solving. Plus, playfulness helps me connect with others and build the relationships that make work worthwhile!"

The Wounded Watchout: "You're going to get hurt if you go around being all playful and making yourself vulnerable. Protect yourself and be on the defensive."
Your Response: "Hey, I know you're trying to protect me, but staying guarded all the time cuts me off from connection and joy. Yes, being playful means letting our guard down, but research shows that vulnerability strengthens relationships and builds trust."

The Cool Police: "Ugh, you're so cringe. No one's going to take you seriously. Just blend in and be cool, okay?"
Your Response: "I get that standing out seems risky, but constantly performing 'cool' is exhausting. The people I actually want in my life value authenticity. I'd rather be free than be cool."

The Responsible Adult: "Playtime is for kids. You have responsibilities now, so start acting like a mature adult."
Your Response: "Being responsible doesn't mean being joyless. Playfulness actually helps me show up better for my

responsibilities—I'm more creative with problems, more patient with challenges, and more energized for what matters."

The Perfectionist: "You can't afford to waste time on play when there's so much pressure to succeed. You can't let yourself make mistakes."
Your Response: "Thanks for trying to protect me from judgment, but research shows that perfectionism actually hampers creativity and innovation. The most successful people embrace playful experimentation and learn from mistakes. It's okay to be imperfect—that's how I grow."

Do any of these sound like the bullies in your brain? If your bully sounds different, give yours a name (as they say, "when we can name it, we can tame it!") and write your own replies to their taunts.

Part of being human is having these fears and doubts. They're not something to resist but something to tinker with. The more we practice responding to our inner critics with warm-spirited energy, the more we can shift the way we relate to ourselves and the world around us.

It's time to stand up for our playful spirits. Now that you're armed with awareness and responses for when the Anti-Play Posse pipes up, let's start playing.

Find Your Wiggle Room
When you're first reconnecting with your playful spirit, you can start small. Try checking your personal lost and found. Journey back to childhood memories and recall what activities once absorbed you completely. What made hours disappear? Perhaps you once loved bouncing on a pogo stick and now running brings that same bodily joy. Maybe you adored playing with dolls and now find pleasure in imagining stories about strangers in the park. Your interests evolve, but the essence of what captivates you often remains.

Now look for today's wiggle room: those small pockets of your life where you feel a bit more at ease and less constricted by expectations. Maybe it's your morning shower, your weekend coffee ritual, or the five minutes before your next meeting.

You might start by simply collecting colors on your morning commute, cracking a joke during a tense moment, or arranging breakfast into a silly face—then suddenly find yourself spotting opportunities for playfulness everywhere, like a contagious laugh spreading through your day and to those around you.

Flexing your play muscles in these small moments lets you experience the power of play at a life-size scale.

Play Takes Guts

Before I send you on, I want to celebrate your courage, because embracing playfulness takes true guts. To be playful means sticking your neck out and being vulnerable in ways that our efficiency-obsessed, judgment-heavy culture often discourages.

Playfulness is an act of rebellion against the pressure to stay in tidy boxes. It's showing up as your authentic self and refusing to contort yourself just to fit in. It means challenging those Anti-Play Posse voices that demand you "act your age," not draw attention, and "be responsible."

Flexing different Powers of Play requires different forms of bravery. The curious person risks looking ignorant as they dare to ask a question, the adventurous soul risks failure as they veer off the well-worn path, the visionary risks being seen as impractical when they imagine opportunities beyond what others can see.

But here's the beautiful secret: Every time you choose playfulness, your courage creates a glimmer. The braver we are, the brighter our lives glow.

When we approach life in this way, we create a field of warmth around us. Playfulness is loving. It's how an irreverent interaction with a complete stranger can envelop you like a hug. Your playful spirit creates unexpected moments of tenderness in a world starved for genuine human contact, helping you deepen relationships with loved ones and create a life rich with meaning and creative collaboration.

DISCOVER YOUR POWERS OF PLAY

YOU ARE PLAYFUL: DISCOVER YOUR SUPER STRENGTHS
Every one of us has natural play powers: ways we bring lightness, creativity, and joy into our lives and the lives of others.

Some of us light up through imagination, others through physical movement, making, or curiosity. Some of us play best alone, others in small groups, still others in active community.

Let's explore the eight Powers of Play I've concocted through research and experience. As you read, notice which ones make you nod in recognition, which remind you of people you love, and which might offer you fresh possibilities for bringing more play into your life.

Think of these powers as trading cards in your personal deck of play possibilities. While you might have a few favorite cards you play most often, they're all on the table for you to pick up.

The goal isn't to limit yourself to one type, but to recognize your natural strengths while trying on other approaches.

POWERS OF PLAY

| The Joyful Jester |

These mischief-makers wield laughter like a magic wand, dissolving tension into connection with a well-timed quip or self-deprecating story. Joyful Jesters know that humor lets us unzip our serious suits when everyone else is armored up. You'll catch them cracking jokes in hospital waiting rooms, finding the absurdity in workplace disasters, or turning family tensions into moments of shared laughter. They're not avoiding difficult realities; they're creating breathing room within them. These playful provocateurs understand that humor can flip power dynamics, speak truth to authority, and create instant bonds between strangers. Their greatest gift? Reminding us that even in our most challenging moments, we can still access joy and that sometimes, our heaviest problems seem more solvable when you infuse them with a little levity.

Powers of Play
- Humor
- Mood shifting
- Tension diffusion
- Social connection

| The Visionary Dreamer |

These imaginative souls float a few feet above the ground, their eyes catching glimpses of what could be while the rest of us are stuck seeing only what is. Visionary Dreamers don't just build castles in the air—they draft the blueprints for bringing them down to earth. You might spot them finding animals in the clouds, reimagining abandoned buildings as future community centers, or turning dinner table conversations into "What if we . . ." brainstorm sessions. For them, imagination goes beyond fantasy. It's the first step toward new realities. They move through the world collecting potential and inviting others into their expansive inner landscapes where anything might just be possible.

Powers of Play
- Imagination
- Innovation
- Future thinking
- World building

| The Adventurous Improviser |

These intrepid spirits are the first to say "Yes, and . . ." when life presents a challenge or unexpected turn. Adventurous Improvisers approach obstacles not as battles to fight but as territories to explore, bringing a refreshing spirit of improvisation to even the most daunting situations. You might find them adapting dinner plans when an ingredient is missing, turning canceled plans into an impromptu gathering, or responding to "this isn't working" with "ok, what if we tried . . ." Whether navigating relationship conflicts or workplace curveballs, Adventurous Improvisers work with what's actually going on rather than clinging to what they wished would happen. They understand that the map is just a suggestion and find exhilaration in charting their way without one.

Powers of Play
- Courageous exploration
- Adaptability
- Spontaneity
- Improvisation

| The Mundane Alchemist |

These playful wizards possess the extraordinary ability to morph the lead of everyday routine into pure gold. Mundane Alchemists don't accept "boring" as a permanent state. It's merely an invitation to shake up their special brand of whimsy. You'll find them turning dish-washing into dance parties, devising elaborate scoring systems for completing expense reports, or adding silly meeting names to brighten up the Google calendar. As these routine remixers entertain themselves, they simultaneously lift the energy of everyone around them, proving that joy doesn't require special occasions. The Mundane Alchemist's workshop is everyday life, where they're constantly tinkering with adding unexpected elements (a dash of competition here, a sprinkle of silliness there) until voilà! The ordinary is newly bedazzled and delightful. They remind us that micro-opportunities for play are all around us, hiding in plain sight.

Powers of Play
- Game design
- Playful problem solving
- Ingenuity
- Rule reinvention

The Expressive Creator

These vibrant makers turn raw materials—whether clay, words, ingredients, or simply the space around them—into expressions of their unique inner landscape. Expressive Creators make things and they make meaning, turning their experiences into tangible creations that help them process and share their perspective. They understand intuitively that creative expression isn't a luxury, but a necessary channel for moving through life's challenges. These artistic players don't require formal training or fancy materials; they simply need the space to transmute what is into something new and beautiful. Whether they're assembling a showstopping outfit, crafting the perfect playlist, or arranging objects into a vignette,

Expressive Creators remind us that we are not passive consumers of our lives—we are its active designers.

Powers of Play
- Artistic creation
- Storytelling
- Visual design
- Space shaping

The Mover and Shaker

These embodied spirits understand a truth many of us have forgotten: our bodies aren't just transportation for our brains—they're instruments of joy, expression, and release. Movers and Shakers communicate through rhythm and motion, finding delight in the simplest physical experiences. You'll catch them suggesting walking meetings when brainstorming sessions stall, shaking off a stressful day with an impromptu living room dance party, or taking the stairs to get their blood pumping with the rhythm of the steps. They intuitively know what research confirms—that movement unlocks creativity, dissolves stress, and connects us to ourselves and others in ways words never could. These kinetic players don't separate "exercise" from "fun." To them, physical movement is one of life's most accessible pleasures. Whether gracefully flowing through yoga poses or enthusiastically jumping into leaf piles, the Mover & Shaker experiences life from the inside out.

Powers of Play
- Physical expression
- Body connection
- Movement
- Energy activation

The Wonder Wanderer

These attentive treasure hunters move through life with the eyes of a beachcomber, spotting the extraordinary within the ordinary that the rest of us rush past. Wonder Wanderers possess the rare ability to experience familiar surroundings as if seeing them for the first time, collecting moments of beauty and surprise like precious shells. You'll find them noticing the geometric patterns in sidewalk cracks, appreciating the perfect symmetry of a sliced bell pepper, or quietly observing how the morning light enlivens a familiar room. As pattern recognizers, they're actively curating their experience, labeling delights as treasures and creating mental collections of life's overlooked wonders. They understand that even in difficult times, the world continues to unfold in beautiful ways if we are aware enough to recognize it.

Powers of Play
- Aesthetic appreciation
- Pattern recognition
- Mindful observation
- Detail collection

The Curious Quester

These inquisitive explorers move through the world with a perpetual "Hmm, I wonder . . ." on the tip of their tongues. Curious Questers approach life as one grand experiment, replacing the pressure of perfection with the liberating mindset of "Let's try it and see." You'll spot them testing new recipes with creative substitutions, asking unexpected questions, or navigating career transitions with a series of small experiments rather than one giant leap. These playful scientists collect data from everyday experiences, turning life's uncertainties into fascinating research questions. They're especially brilliant during in-between times—new parenthood, career changes, relocations—where their "What happens if..." approach recalibrates uncomfortable limbo into rich discovery. The Curious Quester doesn't expect to get things right the first time; they know that each "failure" simply provides more interesting information. Their gift to others? Showing us that not knowing the answer isn't a problem. It's an opportunity for playful investigation.

Powers of Play

- Experimental thinking
- Curiosity
- Discovery drive
- Connection making

As you were introduced to these eight Powers of Play, you might have found yourself vigorously nodding in recognition. Maybe you see yourself in the Wonder Wanderer's keen eye or in the Joyful Jester's knack for finding humor in unexpected places. Maybe you recognized your partner in the Adventurous Improviser's spontaneous spirit, or your best friend in the Mundane Alchemist's contagious game creation.

You're probably not just one type, and you might shift depending on the situation. Maybe you're a Curious Quester at work but a Mover and Shaker at home, or a Visionary Dreamer who channels your Expressive Creator when inspiration hits. These aren't rigid boxes to fit into, but invitations to understand your natural ways of being playful and appreciate others'.

The beauty of understanding your Powers of Play is in the permission it gives you to lean into your natural way of bringing play into the world. When you know that you're a Wonder Wanderer, you might become more confident taking that extra moment to appreciate a beautiful detail. When you recognize your inner Mundane Alchemist, you might be empowered to suggest turning that boring meeting into a creative challenge.

The Powers of Play Go to a Party
Now imagine a party where all our favorite playful powers are present, each expressing their own unique way of bringing joy into the world. The Joyful Jester has a small group in stitches with an impromptu story. The Mover & Shaker has started the dance party and enlisted others to join in the groove. The Wonder Wanderer is noticing snippets of different conversations and how they create accidental poetry, sharing their observations with the person sitting next to them. The Mundane Alchemist has reinvented the food table into a spontaneous taste-testing game, delighting both the social butterflies and the more reserved folks who appreciate having a structure within which to interact. The Adventurous Improviser is rallying folks to go on an unexpected midnight walk, while the Curious Quester is immersed in conversation, diving deep into what started as a casual comment. The Expressive Creator is in a cozy corner playing a drawing game with two other guests while the Visionary Dreamer looks on and imagines what a sight it would be to have hundreds of people in Central Park all drawing at the same time.

See how each player at the party makes the room more vibrant, interesting, and fun?

Which Powers of Play do you see in yourself? In your friends and family? In your colleagues? Understanding different approaches can help us appreciate how others light up the world in their own unique ways and give us new ideas for bringing more play into our own lives.

Notice when they show up in your day-to-day life. Experiment with borrowing moves from different types. Watch how your understanding of your own playfulness deepens and evolves. Remember, there's no wrong way to play—only opportunities to discover new dimensions of joy in your own authentic way.

As we continue our journey through this book, we'll see each Power of Play in action throughout the chapters and how to strengthen them in ourselves through Play Practices.

The Flash Recap: We each have our own natural Powers of Play. These eight powers are trading cards in your deck of possibilities, helping you recognize your strengths while inspiring you to try on new ways of experiencing life.

Wiggle Room: As you move throughout your day, notice any moments when you approach things with curiosity, whimsy, wonder, or silliness.

Play Practice

Superpower Search—Take five minutes to circle your top two Powers of Play. Then jot down one person in your life who embodies a different playful approach you admire. What's their signature move that always makes you smile?

CHAPTER 1

Unzip Your Serious Suit

Loosen up stiff situations with a dose of silliness

Life is far too important a thing to ever talk seriously about.

Oscar Wilde

When tension rises,
we zip up tight

In our Serious Suit,
braced for fight

But don't you feel stiff
up inside that suit?

Are you itching for lightness,
laughter, a hoot?

Take off your armor,
get down to clown

When humor flows,
connection is found

I'm going to say something controversial (here goes!): seriousness gets *way* too much credit for solving problems and addressing difficult situations.

When things get tricky, we often instinctively armor up in our Serious Suits, thinking we have to meet serious situations with serious energy. Like a fighter bracing for a blow, we tighten in times of uncertainty, ready to tussle with the problem.

But here's the twist: that protective suit—our defensive seriousness—actually blocks our superpowers. Like Superman mistakenly suiting up in a kryptonite onesie, our Serious Suit weakens the abilities that come most handy when confronted with challenges: creativity, collaboration, and clear thinking.

Picture this—you're in a tense situation, so you automatically stiffen: crossed arms, tight formal voice, stern posture. It's how you've been taught to take the wheel of control: get serious, show authority. Whether it's a difficult meeting or a child's meltdown, you're following the old map. Your stiffness makes others harden too: Coworkers recoil, kids escalate. By trying to operate from this rigid place, you're losing the camaraderie that could help things flow.

But here's where humor becomes our superpower. Watch what happens when someone dares to be playful in tightly wound moments—whether it's cracking a well-timed joke in a tense meeting or getting silly with an overwhelmed child. Our Joyful Jesters know that rather than losing control, they often gain cooperation by breaking the spell of seriousness. Funnily enough, having the confidence to unzip their Serious Suit and let their guard down shows more strength than wrapping themselves in emotional steel. Their playfulness acts as a release valve, resetting the energy and letting pent-up stress whoosh out of the room.

Picture a tender moment early in dating—you've just said "I love you" for the first time. Instead of the response you hoped for, your partner panics and says something sharp. Ouch. But then they catch themselves: "Wow, I should get the Oscar for worst timing in a romantic movie." You both soften, the tension breaks, and a space is created to talk about what's underneath their response, bringing you closer.

Now imagine being in the ER with a kidney stone, white knuckling your way through waves of pain and panic. Your sibling comes to visit and says "Hey, don't you think this kidney stone needs a proper villain name?" and starts throwing out silly ideas: "Let's call it Kid Vicious! Kidney Lauper! Kid Rock!" You crack up at the absurdity and now you're in it together (plotting against your mutual nemesis) and going into surgery is a little less daunting.

There's something intrinsically vulnerable about being the first one to crack a joke in a tense situation. When we unzip our Serious Suit first, we risk rejection or judgment—maybe no one laughs, maybe they think we're not taking things seriously enough, maybe we misread the room entirely. But that vulnerability is also what makes humor such a powerful bridge builder. When a nurse jokes gently with a scared patient or a leader brings lightness to a stressful meeting, they're extending an invitation. They're saying, "It's safe to be human here." By opening the zipper of their Serious Suit, they're making space for everyone else to breathe a little easier too.

Interestingly, humor has the power to reshape power dynamics. Whether it's a court jester speaking truth to the king through comedy, a child's natural playfulness disarming a rigid adult, or a leader using a self-deprecating joke to connect to their team, humor can flatten the usual hierarchies and level the playing field.

In stuck situations, humor loosens everything up, gets it moving again. While the rest of us are trapped in our stiff combat gear, the person who can stay playful is often the one most agile at navigating the situation, finding the breakthrough solution or building the strongest connections.

The next time you start sliding into your Serious Suit, pause. Notice how constraining it is: How it restricts your breathing, your thinking, your natural warmth. How stiff and itchy it is to be wound so tight. Then try loosening that zipper, just a little bit. Let some air in. Give yourself room to stretch and shimmy. You might find that your light, unguarded self is more powerful than your bulletproof alter ego ever was.

LAUGHTER UNLOCKS BRILLIANCE

Think about how your body reacts when you're under pressure to perform. Your hands likely clench into fists, your jaw tightens, your shoulders bunch up near your ears. You ball up like a freaked-out armadillo. Now try to create something inspired from this strained state. (Yeah, good luck with that!!).

But watch what happens when someone cracks a joke or brings play into the room. Your hands relax, your shoulders drop, your breath deepens. You start to lighten, becoming more buoyant—like a balloon slowly filling with air. In this inflated state, ideas float more freely. Possibilities expand. Your mind has room to play.

I got a window into this truth in my first full-time job out of college at an indie magazine in New York City's SoHo neighborhood. Our office was the antithesis of corporate: a casual, unconventional space hidden above a bar on a cobblestoned street. Here, we were often encouraged to leave our Serious Suits at the door.

Our team's brainstorms were uproarious affairs, filled with a level of psychological safety that I now realize is rare in most workplaces. We weren't afraid to look silly or say something "stupid."

A fly on the wall watching us come up with headline ideas might have thought we were just messing around with our hijinks and silly suggestions. But the creativity generated (and the magazine awards we won as a team) told a different story. As I participated, I noticed a pattern:

Someone would say something ridiculous that made everyone burst out laughing, and then, as we were still quieting our giggles, BOOM! Brilliance: someone would come out with an A+ idea. This pattern repeated itself again and again.

During one session, we were brainstorming headlines for a photo shoot that featured colorful balloon characters dressed up in the season's fashion accessories. We sat down at the round table—that potentially pressured moment where you have to go from no ideas to THE idea. But rather than pressured, it was playful. We warmed up. "Party People!" someone yelled. "Big Poppa!" another chimed in, eliciting appreciative giggles. Ideas started flowing. "Balloon Goons," offered a third person, pushing us along. The energy in the room was palpable, each silly suggestion inflating us more and more until someone shouted "Airheads!" We all doubled over in laughter, and in that moment of pure joy, it happened. "Inflated Egos!" someone exclaimed through tears of laughter. We had our winner.

You'd think more workplaces would catch on to humor's creative power, but I'm constantly amazed by what passes for "brainstorming" in most offices. Usually it's a room full of people (or a Zoom grid) sitting stiffly while their manager announces, "Okay, team, time to be creative!" As if inspiration can be summoned like ordering takeout. Every tentative idea gets hit with "But the budget . . ." or "Well, actually . . ." There's no play, no juice, just a room full of people in their Serious Suits trying to force genius to show up through sheer willpower.

External pressure is often unavoidable—deadlines, standards, and budgets are realities most of us face in our projects. That's why it's so important to carve out pockets for play within the pressure cooker. When we laugh, we hit a reset button on our brains. Stress melts away, our mood lightens, and our minds are free to make unexpected connections. This relaxed state is where creativity thrives, allowing us to see problems from new angles and come up with innovative solutions.

This phenomenon isn't just anecdotal. Students exposed to humor before taking a creativity test came up with more creative solutions than those who didn't get a laugh break. It's as if the laughter allows our minds to expand and inflate (Ziv 1976) whereas stress acts like an imagination blockade.

So the next time you're facing a challenge that requires your best ideas, remember: unzip that Serious Suit. Let yourself inflate like a balloon, buoyed by laughter and play. Create an environment where others feel safe to do the same. Because in that space—where we're not afraid to look foolish, where we can laugh at ourselves and with each other—that's where true brilliance emerges.

SING YOUR ARGUMENTS

When my friend Larz got engaged, a mutual friend invited us to fancy tea to celebrate and asked us to each come prepared to share some relationship advice with the bride-to-be. As we sat eating cucumber sandwiches and drinking strong English tea, people shared classic advice like "Never go to bed angry" (I try not to!) and practical suggestions like making a chore list so you can ensure things are equal.

Then it was my friend Sophia's turn and she surprised us all when she came out with "I suggest singing your arguments!" We all laughed, because of course we did. But Sophia wasn't joking. "For real," she insisted. "When Lawrence and I get mad at each other, we challenge each other to sing the grievances. We have musical arguments!"

She shared how during a road trip to New Mexico, fresh from

watching *Coco* on the plane, they found themselves in a tense moment concerning family dynamics. Instead of letting it simmer, her husband Lawrence started singing to the tune of a *Coco* song, sharing his discomfort with a comment she'd made, reflecting on his own behavior, and expressing his need for her to see his side.

"Something about singing makes it easier to express things we're struggling to admit or understand," Sophia explained. "When you're frustrated but can't quite articulate why, singing lets you be vulnerable without the weight of adult pride. It's like being a kid again—the melody and silliness makes it safe to say the hard stuff."

This playful approach to conflict cracked something open in me. I'd always avoided arguments, seeing them as angsty, scary things where someone wins and someone loses. But this silly, singing approach showed me how they can become creative collaborations where you work through the hard things, not screaming but harmonizing.

Research shows that couples who approach conflict with humor and creativity are more satisfied in their relationships (Walker et al. 2023). It might seem like avoidance, but it's actually finding new ways to move through the hard stuff together. When Sophia and her husband sing their arguments, they're actively rewiring their brains to associate conflict with play instead of threat. I've heard of other couples airing their grievances in Olde English ("Thou hast failed to taketh out the trash, good sir!") or pirate speak ("Arr ye scurvy dog! You've been spending our doubloons like there be treasure buried in every port!") Leaning into absurdity deflates tension while still allowing frustration to be expressed.

We all know that relationships can be really hard. There are fights and tears and moments when there's a chasm between you. In conflict, comedy can be an olive branch. By letting down our guard to find the humor instead of looking for the fight, we open ourselves to the possibility that maybe it's not us against them but just two humans trying to sing in the same key.

CONFLICT TO COMEDY

As any parent (or child!) knows, there's no relationship quite as ripe for conflict or comedy as the parent-child dynamic.

When kids challenge, disobey, or ignore us, we often jump into our Serious Suits. That parental "I mean business!" voice comes out, and suddenly we're playing the role of Strict Parent.

But here's the thing about that Serious Suit: when we stiffen up, our kids often push back harder, creating a cycle that leaves everyone cranky. When we can unzip just a little and bring more levity, we can become better resourced to help our children be cooperative (and stay sane ourselves).

Take my daughter's selective hearing as an example. When she's ignoring me, rather than escalating the power struggle, I'll channel my inner jester and tease, "Oh no! Do you have cotton balls in your ears again?! Let me look for the tweezers so I can pull them out!" This usually elicits a laugh or her playfully rolling her eyes (both vastly superior to the wall of resistance) and then miraculously she'll answer the original question. Reframing the tension as a shared joke amuses us both and helps break the cycle of control and resistance.

This approach works because it appeals to a child's natural desire to play while maintaining the parent's expectations of cooperation and teamwork. When we meet challenges with humor it can create connection instead of opposition.

The beauty of bringing humor into tense situations stretches far beyond parenting. Whether you're dealing with a stubborn toddler or a difficult colleague, the principle remains the same: humor can be like a magic key that unlocks stuck situations.

Of course humor can go sideways when misdirected, so please—I implore you!—don't use it to mock, belittle, or dismiss real concerns. The goal is to ease tension and create connection, not avoid important issues or make fun. Jest thoughtfully.

You might offer up a witty observation of the situation at hand that speaks truth with levity ("We're all just trying to look competent here"). Or playfully state the obvious ("Well, this is awkward . . ."). Or you crack a joke about yourself, putting vulnerability on the table for all present ("My inner control freak has entered the chat"). Or you might deliver an absurd analogy that is just silly enough to disarm and shift the mood ("Are we polishing the brass on a sinking ship, here?").

Next time tension arises, find the funny. By looking for comedy in conflict, you might just find that a moment of shared laughter creates the opening for true collaboration to flow through.

SERIOUS TIMES CALL FOR SERIOUS HUMOR

Most situations aren't as serious as we make them out to be. They're not life-and-death. But even in high-stakes situations, humor can be a powerful tool. In the ER, teams of nurses and doctors often use playful humor and lightness to ease the stress, help create trust with patients, and keep their minds agile enough to find solutions.

I got a window into how this works, when I met Carley Brew, an ER nurse at a nonprofit hospital in Florida. "You have to have humor in my job," she told me. "It's such a great way to maintain peace among patients and create a positive environment."

Carley explained that when she walks into a patient's room, she always cracks little jokes to show that she and her patient are on the same team. When patients are stiff and guarded, they might not be forthcoming with the critical information she needs to treat them, so she uses humor to relate, loosen things up, and get patients to be vulnerable enough to share what's really going on. "I have to know everything about you to save you," she says. Through jokes and building rapport, she creates a friendly, open dynamic that improves her ability to care for patients, and how patients treat her in return.

She'll start with a joke about her height because patients often comment on how tall she is. So, as she's raising someone's bed, she might say, "Look, I didn't realize I was tall until I came down to Florida. Now I go to the bar and I can see who's bald." Her go-to jokes work wonders. Suddenly "the room isn't as stuffy. It's a little more breathable." Carley's got a trove of dad jokes that she reaches for regularly to help her do her job.

When a patient's anxiety is spiking their heart rate, they're hyperventilating, and their panic is making their symptoms worse. So she'll look at them and say, "Listen, don't panic unless I'm panicking. When I'm panicking you can do whatever you want. But right now I'm not panicking, so I need you to breathe. We got this. You're doing great." This approach often gets a smile. It's her way of observing the situation, bringing the patient's awareness into the moment, and putting them on the same team.

Research shows why this works: Positive humor reduces cortisol (our primary stress hormone) while activating multiple regions of the brain simultaneously, enhancing our ability to find solutions (Kramer and Leitao 2023). When we laugh, our bodies release endorphins and dopamine, counteracting stress responses that can narrow our thinking (Berk et al. 2001).

With more serious patients who don't respond to humor, Carley shifts to curiosity and rapport-building by finding things they have in common. Any way to get closer on a human level is advantageous for her job.

The ER is a scary place. People are dying all the time. Carley can go from a room where she just lost a patient to one where someone just arriving needs her full attention. She wants to go into that new room with a smile on her face. Humor among the staff is a coping mechanism, a way to release stress, process trauma, and keep moving. It's not making light per se or negating the hurt, it's finding life within horror, levity within seriousness, and staying present and engaged in the work at hand.

Of course, comedy can be risky and we often avoid it because we don't want to hurt or offend someone (especially if they're already suffering). Carley stresses reading the room before cracking a joke. An intense active emergency is usually not the right place for jokes—if someone has a gunshot wound or needs to be resuscitated, Carley and the medical staff are solely focused on saving their life. But once the immediate danger is past, levity can offer welcome relief for all the built-up anxiety. The key is knowing when and how to deploy humor in sensitive situations. As with a skilled nurse, timing and precision matter.

Humor shouldn't be used at someone's expense or used to deflect from real issues. Used effectively (like with her panic example), it can actually bring more awareness to a tough moment, if delivered with levity. It works best when it highlights our shared humanity or the universal absurdity of difficult moments.

As Carley shows us, those who maintain their sense of playfulness in challenging times aren't just more pleasant to be around—they can be more effective problem solvers and stronger leaders. By unzipping our Serious Suits even in the most serious situations, we help ourselves burn off stress so we can problem solve and connect with people in the moment.

THE RIDICULOUS RESISTANCE

When I was in college, I hitched a ride to Washington, D.C., with a group of absurdist protesters to rally against the Iraq War. While thousands marched with serious signs, I showed up dressed as a bloody Exxon cheerleader, pom-poms and all, chanting corporate-sounding slogans about oil profits. Years later, I'd join a dancing conga line protesting New York's archaic cabaret laws that banned dancing in bars. More recently, I volunteered with Joy to the Polls, which brought DJs and performers to polling places to counter voter intimidation with celebration.

Activists call this approach tactical frivolity: a term that gained popularity in the 1990s to describe protests that use humor, absurdity, and carnival-like antics to challenge power. When you show up to something heavy with something light, you disarm people. Absurdity reveals the absurdity already baked into the system.

Playful protest might seem silly, but it's about refusing to let the heaviness of injustice crush the spirit required to fight it. When you bring joy to resistance, you're modeling the world you're fighting for as fierce and funny, angry and alive, determined and dancing all at once.

The jester knows what the king doesn't: sometimes the best way to reveal an ugly truth is to dress it up in bells and make people laugh at it.

WE LAUGH SO WE DON'T CRY (BUT WE CRY TOO)

"When things are so sad, you need humor and levity," says Kate Thompson, a New York–based therapist who has experienced this truth twice over—first at fifteen when she lost her mom to cancer, and again recently with her dad's passing.

Humor was her dad's way of moving through the hardest things, including his wife's terminal illness. Growing up with seven siblings, he learned early how laughter could shift tough moments. Even during Kate's mom's final days, he found ways to bring lightness through gentle observations that honored both the gravity and the absurdity of their situation.

There's an unspoken rule that grief should be handled with unwavering solemnity. But at her mom's funeral, Kate found herself waiting with her brothers in the church vestibule. The boys were dressed in suits their mom had personally picked out—a touching but comical sight since her brothers never wore formal wear. As they waited for their dad, the boys shrugged off their suit jackets, dangled them on a finger over one shoulder, and started an impromptu fashion show, strutting and posing in front of the church. It was silly and sacred at once: honoring their mom's final act of dressing them up while letting themselves be playful even in their pain. A moment of relief and release on a brutal day.

Years later, when her dad passed away, fashion shows again became an unexpected vehicle for processing grief. The task of packing up her dad's clothes to donate was weighing on Kate. Then, one evening, while giving her seven-year-old son a bath in her dad's bathroom, she turned the overwhelming task into a celebration, pulling out each carefully chosen piece from her dad's wardrobe (the race shirts from the 1980s with their retro mesh, the overalls he wore every weekend after her mom passed), and presented these treasured artifacts to her son with little prompts and questions. This shirt or that? Where do you think grandpa wore this? How many used tissues do you think are in this jacket pocket? She added laughter to what could have been a solitary, heavy task.

The fashion show tradition reached its peak during a pre-planned family beach trip to the Outer Banks, a vacation her dad hadn't lived to join. Instead of letting grief overshadow the trip, the family went to a thrift store where everyone accepted the challenge to pick out outfits under $20 to model in the family fashion show. They each chose their entrance music, then took turns emerging to prance and pose in their looks. "We laughed so hard," Kate remembers. "It wasn't something we'd ever done with Dad, but he would have thought it was so amazing. We still let ourselves be sad, but we were also really silly."

As a therapist, Kate is thoughtful about when and how to use humor around grief. "Within a family it can work really well because you know each other so intimately," she explains. "But you need permission to make something into a joke and it doesn't always land." Sometimes a gentle observation or self-deprecating comment can test the waters before diving deeper into comedic relief.

"People think of grief as just sadness," Kate explains, "but it's all sorts of emotions. Silliness and humor are part of that too." The fashion shows were about letting joy exist alongside the pain, knowing that even in our deepest grief, life and love continue to bubble up.

"People get caught up in the end—'Oh, they were so sick, those last days were so rough,'" Kate says. "Fuck that. I want to think of my dad in 1986 wearing short shorts while mowing the lawn. I want to remember him when he was really alive, when he could laugh."

By finding moments of levity in loss, we honor not just our grief but the joy and humor that made our loved ones who they were. We unzip our Serious Suits enough to let in the full range of emotions that come with loving and losing someone. And sometimes, in sharing a laugh through tears, we find ourselves most deeply connected to both the people we've lost and those still by our side.

* * *

From boardrooms to hospital rooms, we see how levity breaks through tension, sparks creative thinking, and builds bridges between people. Comedy is a strategic tool for dealing with life shenanigans. So, notice when you're squeezing into your Serious Suit, grab the zipper, and slide it down to let in some air.

Sometimes even a small unzip of our Serious Suits helps us to recognize that playfulness is powerful, even (especially!) in serious situations. That maybe being playful would deliver more than worrying about being taken seriously ever did. Start small, stay kind, and notice how a little lightness can lead to breakthrough moments.

Life's too short and too wonderfully absurd to spend wrapped in rigidity and formality. So go ahead, unzip that Serious Suit and let your inner jester out to play.

Your "Unzip Your Serious Suit" Toolkit
Develop Your Joyful Jester Powers

The Flash Recap: Humor breaks through the barriers that seriousness can't budge. Though our instinct may be to armor up when conflict arises, a dose of levity can crack open stuck situations and bring unexpected breakthroughs.

Humor cuts tension, not by making light of serious issues (though most issues are not as serious as we make them), but by helping everyone's brain relax enough to think more clearly and creatively.

Wiggle Room: Whenever you catch yourself holding tension today, intentionally drop your shoulders and soften your jaw. This tiny physical "unzipping" creates a little space for playfulness to enter.

Play Practice
Find the Funny

Replay serious moments through a humorous lens

This practice puts you in the director's chair of your life, turning daily drama comedic.

How to Practice

Each evening, pick one moment in the day where you got all serious and zipped up. Then ask: "What if this were a comedy scene instead?"

Ways to Find the Funny

- Spot the ridiculous detail: What was weirdly specific or absurd about the situation?
- Find your cartoon moment: What would it look like as a dramatic doodle with a caption?
- Give it an episode name: How would you describe this to a friend to make them laugh?
- Sensationalize it: Dial up the drama to a ten.
- Find the universal human truth: What does this say about how bizarre human behavior is?
- Notice: Today's taking myself too seriously moment was ...

Try scribbling it in your journal, doodling it as a comic strip, telling someone who will find it entertaining, or just shaking your head and chuckling about it by yourself. Remember: it's not about minimizing real emotions or making everything funny. Some moments may not be ready for a laugh track, and that's A-OK too.

The cool thing is that by doing this practice in the rearview mirror, we prep ourselves for finding levity in real time, catching ourselves mid–Serious Suit and saying: "Wait, what's funny here?"

"Impossible!" "Preposterous!"
"No way!" they say

As if wilder things don't
happen each day

Our existence itself on
this spinning rock

A miracle, marvel,
a wonderful shock

So believe in potential
and imagine away

Build with your dreaming
tomorrow's gateway

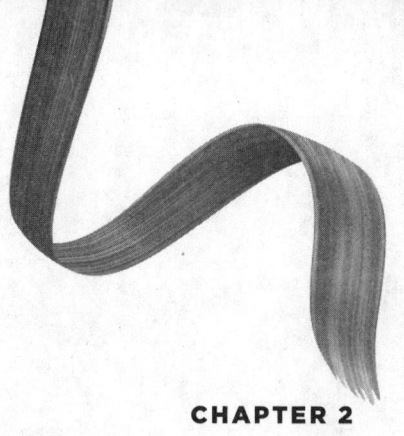

CHAPTER 2

Look for Pink Flamingos

Get real about imagination and open new worlds of possibility

Imagination allows you to bend the rules of the temporal world.

Amy Sherald

Remember when a cardboard box was a soaring spaceship, a royal castle, and a pirate's ship all in one afternoon? When the living room floor was bubbling hot lava that could only be crossed by leaping from couch to ottoman? That wild, magical thinking went beyond mere child's play—it was a super strength that let us explore infinite realms, solve problems, and envision new opportunities that didn't yet exist.

But somewhere between learning algebra and getting our first job, many of us traded that exuberant, anything-is-possible vision for a more "practical" mindset. As our analytical thinking grew, we went from "what if" dreaming to "what is" logic.

The good news: Our brains remain flexible throughout our lives. We can form new neural pathways and reawaken dormant ones (Zanto and Gazzaley 2019). Our thinking may have changed and become more practical, but our imagination isn't gone—it's just waiting for us to reopen our doorway to dreaming.

Every scientific breakthrough, every work of art, every positive change started with someone imagining what could be. In our rapidly changing world, we need our Visionary Dreamer power more than ever. Fantastical thinking serves as a gateway to finding new solutions for complex challenges, allowing us to both escape reality and expand it. Time to dust off that cardboard box!

LOOKING FOR PINK FLAMINGOS IN BROOKLYN

On a balmy June morning, I tried to motivate my daughter, Viva, to walk with momentum down our block in Brooklyn. We were already twenty minutes late to a friend's brunch.

Have you ever tried to go somewhere with a toddler? It's slow going! Everything intrigues and distracts them—the shiny candy wrapper on the ground, the colorfully dressed neighbor walking by, the plastic bag stuck in the tree. It's two steps forward, ten steps back as they chase a dog down the street. This awareness and curiosity is beautiful in many ways, *but* sometimes we have a destination to get to, an adult timeline we're on, and we want to CLAP! OUR! HANDS! and scream "Come on! Let's gooooooooooooooo!"

As usual, Viva was dillydallying, playing sidewalk inspector and closely observing a planting of peach-colored peonies outside our building.

I had already told Viva that we needed to hurry, but lateness doesn't register with a two-year-old. In this moment, I could feel the pressure building in my body.

I searched for ways to motivate her beyond the ten-foot radius of our home.

An idea popped into my head: I thought she might respond to the prospect of finding something wild and unexpected in our urban environment, so I blurted out, "Hey, Viva, let's see if we can find some pink flamingos! I think there might be some closer to Ray Ray's house." Pink flamingos seemed exciting and fun and, of course, pink. Viva loved pink. I held my breath for a beat, trying to play it cool. She took the bait.

Viva looked up at me, her face so open and eager, then started to bounce up and down excitedly, like a baby bird. I grabbed her hand, and she picked up the pace as we headed down the block. I, of course, knew there were no pink flamingos on the next block or the one after (we live in Brooklyn, after all) but I thought the hunt for them might be motivational—and it was turning out to be!

Now that her little black Vans were slapping the pavement, we passed a converted warehouse building and the deli with all its brightly colored sandwich signs, and rounded the corner past the plant shop. Viva tugged my arm as she walked with purpose, head held high, alert and looking for flamingos.

As we crossed the sidewalk, hand in hand, I was preoccupied thinking about what I would say to our host about our tardy arrival.

All of a sudden, my daughter shouted out with glee, "FAMINGOS!" I looked toward where her chubby little hand was pointing and, to my utter surprise, there were six pink flamingos (plastic, but still!) in the yard of one of the walk-up apartments that lined the block. I stopped in my tracks gobsmacked, but Viva yanked me closer to inspect them.

Viva was delighted. I was delighted, but then I felt dismayed by the limits of my imagination. I had set us off on this mission without truly believing we'd find tropical birds (real or plastic) on the streets of New York City.

However, to search for flamingos in Brooklyn was an entirely reasonable pursuit for my toddler. And she had found them!

Oh me of little faith! I had fallen for the oldest trick in the adult playbook: I'd stopped believing in the "impossible."

You may be thinking, "So what?!" And yeah, perhaps this example doesn't seem consequential because there's nothing urgently important about being open to finding flamingos. But what about staying open to finding love? Or believing that you're worthy of your dream project? Or thinking we could find climate solutions?

When we say "There's no way" or "I could NEVER," we close out a treasure trove of solutions and opportunities.

What we believe to be possible shapes what we actually experience. When we open our consciousness to unexpected options, we often discover that reality is more magical than we imagined. The only way to find pink flamingos (our official bird of possibility!) is to imagine they could be out there and to go looking for them.

IMAGINARY CLUB-HOPPING

Life had shrunk to the size of my apartment. We were in the midst of COVID and we were struggling—lonely, disconnected, grateful to be alive but not exactly bubbling with vivaciousness.

With the hope of socializing and sparking joy, I decided to invite people to join me for virtual play sessions with guided creative exercises and visualizations.

As faces pop up in their little Zoom boxes, I see the weariness in their eyes, the tension in their shoulders. But there is something else too—a glimmer of anticipation, a readiness to be transported. "Okay," I say, trying to infuse my voice with a commanding, cheerful energy that feels foreign after so much time in isolation. "Tonight, we're going club-hopping."

A few eyebrows raise. The idea of "going" anywhere seems absurd when we are all stuck in our homes.

"Close your eyes," I instruct. A few do immediately. Others hesitate, glancing around to see who else is playing along. Eventually, all the faces on my screen have their eyes shut.

As Rhye's "Feel Your Weight" starts playing, I begin: "You're walking down the street in New York with good friends. It's nighttime and the city lights are twinkling. You pulse with the electric sense of potential that comes with a night out."

I guide them through the street, into a club where they are whisked past the red velvet rope. I describe the hazy colored lights, the press of the crowd, the clasp of a friend's hand as they weave through the throng. "Now you're in a room with a light-up dance floor," I continue, my own mental movie rolling. "It changes colors with each step you take. You move through a heart-shaped glowing tunnel, and suddenly you're in a trampoline room. Now your child self comes into the room, they clasp your hand, and jump up and down with you."

As I speak, I notice a shift. I peek at the screen, notice how furrowed brows relax. Shoulders drop away from ears. Soft smiles start to bloom.

In our mind's eye, we climb a narrow staircase to an outdoor balcony with a swing. The moon rises overhead as we settle onto the swing and swoosh through the night sky, heads tilted to the stars, feeling the wind in our hair. With each new scene, I feel farther from the claustrophobic walls of my home and closer to the pre-pandemic life I missed so dearly.

When I finally ask everyone to open their eyes, the faces that look back at me are reawakened. Eyes brighter, bodies looser.

"How do you feel?" I ask.

The responses flood in. "I wanted to stay there at the club!" "I loved feeling free." "That was the absolute most fun." One woman shared happy tears emojis and said: "I forgot about everything. I felt alive again."

In that fantasy nightclub, we discovered that our minds are boundless even when our physical world is limited. Research corroborates what we viscerally experienced: when we vividly conjure scenes, our brains respond almost as if we are experiencing real ones—releasing endorphins, reducing anxiety, and giving us a sense of control. It's why "think of your happy place" is common advice when in a stressful situation and why losing ourselves in a great novel or film can be so affecting.

During those long lockdown days, as we all grappled with a world turned upside down, we found that even when we can't control our external circumstances, we can still explore our inner landscape and find space to soar.

PLAYING PRETEND MAKES US PREPARED

But imagination isn't just an escape hatch from reality—it can also be a road map to it. When we dream, we can mentally rehearse, creating new neural pathways that prepare us for new experiences. Visualization is a tool used by top performers across fields—from athletes to organizers to musicians—who employ it to practice and role-play different scenarios.

Scientists found that people who visualized practicing a new piano exercise showed similar neural activity as those who physically rehearsed (Meister et al. 2004). The mental practice alone improved their playing ability (Bernardi et al. 2013). Their brains couldn't tell the difference between the imagined and real preparation.

When Carina Sherman first started DJing as Fluid Alien, they used imagination as their dress rehearsal space. "On bus rides, or lying awake at night, I'd picture the crowd, the lights, and how one track would melt into the next," they told me. "Before my first official gig, I stood alone in my apartment and pretended there was an audience. I felt the energy, I even felt the goosebumps."

By the time their real debut arrived, they weren't in unknown territory—it was déjà vu. "It looked and felt exactly as I had pictured," they said, "only louder, brighter, and more alive."

This is the practical magic of imagination.

BUILDING DREAM WORLDS

A decade ago, my team at Refinery29 was tasked with an exciting challenge: to create an unforgettable experience to celebrate our company's ten-year anniversary. As our executive creative director, I rallied our team to start brainstorming and asked them to bring stories of the most memorable nights of their lives for us to draw inspiration from. They came with tales of underground parties, fantastical art exhibitions, and experiences rich with discovery, spontaneity, and wonder.

From those stories emerged a wild idea. What if we took over a warehouse and built a funhouse of style, culture, and creativity with twenty-nine different spaces? We could create each space in collaboration with different creators, brands, or culture shapers. It would bring our digital content to life in a way no one had seen before. We'd call it 29Rooms.

When we presented the idea, the leadership team's interest was piqued. Then practicality crashed down. I felt my stomach drop as a barrage of logistical questions and doubts came my way: "Could we really get thousands of people to come?" "Why would brands want to take part?" "What exactly is in these rooms?" Then an exec said: "Maybe we should just have a cocktail party." The words hit the conference room like a pin to a balloon. (A cocktail party! How innovative!)

As the creative leader who championed this vision, I felt the weight of everyone's skepticism pressing down on me. Maybe they were right. Maybe it was too risky, too ambitious, too weird an idea.

But something inside me refused to give up. The team and I retreated to tackle the hard questions, knowing we needed to transform our abstract idea into something others could see and believe in.

A breakthrough came on the taxi ride to look at a warehouse space. As the city whizzed by our windows, our creative director, project manager, and I started to paint in the specific details of the event. "What if we had a drive-in cinema room where we screened women-directed films?" I floated. "What if there's a dress-up den?" Theresa suggested. "And a lipstick mirror maze sponsored by a beauty brand!" Albie dreamed out loud. With each "what if," the vision got clearer and more real. We could see it, feel it, step inside it.

When we arrived at the warehouse, we climbed up to the second floor and stopped dead in our tracks. There, stretching along the hallway, were twenty-nine rooms, lined up in a row, ready to be filled with our visions.

Armed with our new vivid picture (and the perfect space to make it come to life), we went back to leadership and painted the sensory-rich scene: "You'll arrive at a warehouse and wonder, 'where the hell am I?' then see a technicolor mural leading to a rainbow-lit staircase. You'll enter a glitter lips doorway, go into a *2001: A Space Odyssey*–style VR room done in partnership with a tech brand . . ." We made them the passengers in our dream mobile and now they were looking out the window and could see what we saw.

Six months later, when we opened our doors, lines stretched around the block. Adults moved through the space like giddy children—mouths agape, skipping, exploring. In the silent disco people danced under black lights as Day-Glo feathers floated in the air. Rainbow doorways drew visitors from room to room, each space sparking wonder and play.

As I took in the miraculous scene, a visitor grabbed my hand and gushed: "this space made me want to start dreaming bigger." When we dare to make our wildest visions real, we give other people permission to expand their own sense of what's possible too.

IF JUST 3.5 PERCENT OF US BELIEVE

> People be like "that's not realistic" as if the
> entire universe is not a living miracle beyond
> our wildest imagination.
> *James McCrae*

I was sitting in a bustling café in Union Square with my friend Sophia Li, a journalist and climate advocate who radiates optimism like she has sunshine flowing through her veins. We were talking about the state of the world (you know, light conversation for a Tuesday morning) and whether she thought playfulness had a role in solving big problems.

"Look, the scale of challenge we face is immense," she said. "But if we keep being doom and gloom, saying it's a 'dumpster fire,' we'll get mired in that pessimistic belief and inaction. We have to remember that imagination actually makes us more human, more empathetic, better problem solvers. It lets us step into other people's shoes. We think play is all lighthearted fun, but it actually removes roadblocks to help us be more unified as a collective."

I sighed and said, "It just seems so hard."

Sophia's eyes twinkled. "Let me tell you about the three-point-five percent rule," she said. She told me about Harvard professor Erica Chenoweth, who studied 323 civil resistance campaigns over the last century, including the Philippines' Freedom Movement and the South African antiapartheid movement. Her discovery: it only takes the active and sustained participation of 3.5 percent of a population to create serious social change.

Think about that. Just 3.5 percent of people, dreaming up a different existence and acting on it. That's all it takes to reshape the world.

Before any change happens in the real world, it has to happen in our minds. We have to dream about what could be before we can create it. We walk around with invisible boxes, built from our past experiences, our biases, our fears—the voice that says, "That'll never work," or "Things have always been this way."

These boxes excuse us from trying and risking disappointment or sounding "crazy." But the boxes? They're imaginary. We built them, which means we have the power to break them down and build a new existence beyond them.

* * *

The next time you notice yourself throttling what you believe is possible by trying to "be realistic," remember that dreaming is a reality expander. Whether you're doing dress rehearsals in your mind, escaping to imaginary clubs when your spirit needs a boost, or envisioning solutions that don't yet exist, imagination allows us to get over our passive acceptance of what is and become the architects of what could be.

Your "Looking for Pink Flamingos" Toolkit
Develop Your Visionary Dreamer Powers

The Flash Recap: Our imaginations are powerful tools for rejuvenation, preparation, and resilience. When we dare to envision what could be, we often discover that reality is more expansive than we assumed. By staying open to potential, we can strengthen this uniquely human super strength.

Wiggle Room: If you catch yourself thinking "That's impossible" or "That would never work," pause. Take a breath. Ask yourself, "What if it were possible? What would that look like?"

Play Practice
Coffee Cup Portal

Use your morning routine to stretch your imagination

Start each day with a small mental stretch, by using your coffee/tea ritual to prime your brain to search for possibility.

How to Practice

1. Sit with your morning beverage and take three easy breaths.
2. Look into your cup and imagine it's a portal.
3. Choose one portal option from below to visualize.
4. Close your eyes and briefly imagine the scene in detail.
5. Open your eyes, return to the present, and take your first sip.

Portal Options

- Future Self: Picture yourself at a future date celebrating achieving something you're working toward
- Time Travel: Revisit a childhood space that brought you joy or comfort
- Coffee Date: Imagine having coffee with someone you miss or want to connect with
- Past Self: Envision having coffee with your past self. What do you want to tell yourself?
- Adventure: Transport to a place you want to see

Know that different brains imagine in different ways: You might see vivid details, need to use words to build the scene, or just feel a gentle sense of possibility. There's no right or wrong way. The goal is to gently expand your mind beyond the confines of your current reality, opening up new opportunities in your day.

When life surprises,
don't suit up for a fight

Rigid resistance keeps
joy out of sight

Say "Yes, and" to what
each moment brings

Turn challenges to open,
curious things

Improvise freely,
trade pressure for play

Calling you to practice
the Playful Way

CHAPTER 3

Practice the Playful Way

Flex your improv muscles to face challenges and roll with change

Play is training for the unexpected.

Marc Bekoff

Once upon a time my mom read me a classic Aesop's fable, and it's stuck with me since childhood. It goes a little something like this: On a windy day, an oak tree side-eyes a neighboring reed with pity. The oak is standing proud, upright and strong in the wind, while the reed is waving around, bending low and bobbing back up as the gusts of air blow.

The oak thinks to itself, "Wow, look at that wimpy reed flopping around, I'm so much stronger, holding firm like a boss!"

But then a nasty hurricane comes. The oak is rigid and unyielding, holding strong, while the reed does its bendy dance in the wild wind.

When the storm passes, guess who's left standing? The flexible reed stands unharmed and the "mighty" oak has toppled, roots in the air.

I love how this story flips the script on strength. We're taught to "be unwavering" and "stand our ground," but there's great advantage in knowing when to sway and bend. Adventurous Improvisers know that flexibility is the wisest strength in a turbulent world.

IMPROVISING PAST PANIC

I used to nearly black out from the stress of public speaking. I'd over-prepare obsessively, memorizing a script by repeating it over and over again. Then, when I'd get in front of people, the pressure to perfectly deliver my lines would put me in a state of panic, and when, inevitably, something would be different from how I'd prepped, I'd completely draw a blank on how to respond. Onstage, I'd rush to get it over with, floating out of my body. An unexpected question might cause my mind to go completely blank, or a technical error could untether me from my flow, causing me to trip over my words. Once I was done, the experience would flash back painfully and I'd find myself dissecting everything I got wrong, picking my performance apart and flushing with shame.

As a spokesperson for my company, I had to face this fear often.

There was a lot that I wanted to say, a lot of interesting work to share, but the pressure of public speaking made me freeze up, and I just couldn't find the joy in it.

Our communications team connected me with a media trainer to help me get more comfortable on stage. I was excited to finally break through this professional barrier and I set to work with the trainer, whom I'll call Derek, a tall guy with a serious demeanor. Derek filmed me practicing a talk. When I was done, he shook his head from side to side. It was clear he felt I was going to be *quite* the project. He played back the recording and pointed out everything I was doing wrong: every rushed line, each "um" and "like," every time I swayed. Derek pointed to the paused tape: "See here? When you get excited you do that chaotic movement with your hands. It's like you have raptor claws." I looked at my hands in dismay.

To show me how it should be done, he played clips of professional speakers with considered, choreographed hand gestures that corresponded to what they were saying, delivered right on cue.

I took it all in and tried harder, preparing extra for the next session, diligently trying to avoid my errors and memorize my hand gestures, pauses, and walking cues. I tried to step into this role of "professional speaker." When we had our next rehearsal, the pressure to perform felt even higher and, despite my practice, I still said "um," made ungraceful gestures, and rushed. I got just as many notes on what I was doing wrong and needed to change. While I was grateful to have access to a trainer, I felt defeated and like I needed a different kind of help. Instead of being trained out of all my technical errors and molded into someone I was not, I wanted someone who could help me get more comfortable expressing *myself*, connecting with the audience, and rolling with surprises.

In the meantime, an idea for a talk that I'd submitted to South by Southwest—the renowned media conference in Austin—had been selected, meaning I was on deck for a big keynote. I knew I needed to ditch the pressure of being perfect and focus instead on courageously being present with the audience, having fun, and being generous with my knowledge and energy. I wondered how I could show the audience the joyful self that I was in my day-to-day interactions with my team, friends, and family. I shared those goals with a colleague, who suggested I try improv classes and also connected me with a pair of theater coaches, Casey and Erin, two exuberant women dressed colorfully.

The improv classes could not have had a more different vibe from the media training. A core principle of improv is saying "Yes, and"—you accept whatever happens and build on it. Instead of fighting surprises, you work with them.

We did exercises like "be a pretend expert," where we drew a random topic out of a hat (dinosaurs, shoes, air-conditioning units) and had to talk for two minutes as though we were the world expert on the topic, delivering a lecture to the class. The games we played in class were practice for thinking on our toes, being present, and trusting ourselves. They gave me space to playfully experiment with how I communicated, with both words and gestures, and helped build confidence in my spontaneity. Rather than stuffing myself into a "professional speaker" box, I found myself gleefully alive in expression.

With the big keynote on the horizon, I started practicing these new skills in my monthly team meeting, seeing if I could come without notes, turn a typo into an opportunity for a joke, if I could observe the audience to find a moment to connect, and laugh at my mistakes and keep going. What happened was that I started to see the unexpected—the technical glitches, interruptions, mistakes—as opportunities to riff, to find levity, and to be more human. I began to relish the opportunities to improvise!

When the South by Southwest keynote came, I still had Derek's voice in my head and feared flopping. But I knew I was prepared. I gave myself the gift of going up without notes so that I could be more present and improvisational. To help me shrug off my nerves,

I had the audience do an improv shake-out with me, flailing our arms and legs while counting down five, four, three, two, one. I felt the energy in the room lift and my own confidence grow. I found the people in the audience who were leaning forward in their seats and nodding and made eye contact with them, anchoring myself in the connection. When the sound on one of the videos in my presentation didn't work, I riffed a voice-over and sang the music, eliciting laughs. I had the best time I'd ever had giving a talk, and when I was done, I got a standing ovation. Later that day, the conference organizer called and asked me to do a repeat performance the next day due to high interest. I was thrilled.

Whereas the strict, serious, diligent approach had failed, the silly, playful, improvisational approach had helped me not only succeed but find joy in the process. I experienced how when we're faced with challenges, we can choose—the Pressured Way or the Playful Way.

THE PRESSURED WAY OR THE PLAYFUL WAY

The Pressured Way	The Playful Way
Fighting against the problem	Saying "Yes, and"
Resistant	Accepting
Defensive	Receptive
Seeking control	Open to experimentation
One "Right" answer	Many possible solutions
Forcing	Exploratory
Self critical	Self compassionate
Rigid / Strict	Flexible / Fluid
In your head	In the moment
Competition	Collaboration
Zero Sum Thinking	Abundant mindset

When faced with a new challenge, change, or the unforeseen, our instinct is often to dig in our heels and try to control everything. But this rigid response—while perfectly human—often cuts us off from creative solutions. In those moments, we have a choice that most of us don't realize we're making. We can take the Pressured Way or the Playful Way.

We're often conditioned to take the Pressured Way: to approach obstacles with grim determination, to muscle through resistance, and to view compromise as weakness. The old story says that for someone to win, someone else has to lose. But the Playful Way offers a liberating alternative—one where creativity, connection, and collaboration replace control, competition, and conquest.

At the heart of the Playful Way is the improvisational principle of "Yes, and"—accepting what's happening rather than fighting against it, then building upon that reality generatively. When we say "No" or "Yes, but," we kill the idea flow. Similarly, when we take the Pressured Way, we fight against our challenges, trying to negate or resist them.

Embracing "Yes, and" doesn't mean passive resignation; it means collaborating with what's happening instead of fighting it (which opens up space for clever solutions). When we say yes to our circumstances and then ask, "And what can I create from here?" we reframe challenges as opportunities.

The Pressured Way is similar to what psychologists call psychological inflexibility—getting stuck to specific outcomes. Research shows this mindset limits our ability to adapt to changing circumstances and contributes to increased stress and decreased well-being (Hayes et al. 2006).

The Playful Way, by contrast, aligns with psychological flexibility, or rolling with whatever comes your way by adapting and shifting your perspective (Kashdan and Rottenberg 2010). This adaptable mindset enables us to bend without breaking when life's squalls hit us.

When we choose to take the Playful Way—the improvisational,

accepting, exploratory way—we pick a warmer, fuzzier, more elastic way of being in the world.

FINDING YOUR "YES, AND"

Improvisers train to respond creatively to whatever happens onstage, developing the same muscles we need to navigate life's inevitable changes with grace and creativity, the Playful Way.

The principles of improvisation, pioneered by Viola Spolin (often called "the mother of improv") in the 1930s, weren't originally designed for entertainment. Spolin developed these techniques as a social worker helping immigrant children adapt to new environments. What began as a way to help people navigate unfamiliar circumstances evolved into powerful tools for anyone facing change or uncertainty.

What can improvisers teach us about finding our own spirit of play when facing life's curveballs?

Stay in the present moment. Improvisers can't plan their next line while their scene partner is speaking or they'd miss crucial information. Similarly, when we're fully present with our challenges rather than catastrophizing about the future, we notice details, opportunities, and resources we might otherwise miss.

Treat mistakes as gifts. In improv, there are no mistakes, only unexpected offers. When someone misplaces a prop, it becomes part of the scene. What if we approached life's disruptions with the same curiosity? Who knows? That canceled flight might lead to a conversation with a stranger who becomes a friend.

Make your partner look good. Improvisers focus on supporting each other rather than stealing the spotlight. In life's challenges, this means asking, "How can I contribute to a solution that works for everyone?" rather than just protecting your own interests.

Trust the process. Improvisers step onstage without knowing what will happen, trusting that something interesting will emerge if they follow these principles. Similarly, when we trust our ability to adapt rather than needing to control outcomes, we discover solutions we couldn't have planned.

These principles are mindsets that help us shift rigid thinking into flexible responsiveness. By practicing them in small, low-stakes situations (like traffic jams or technology glitches), we build our capacity to bring this Adventurous Improviser spirit to bigger life changes.

When you find yourself tightening up against change, try asking: "What would an improviser do right now?" The answer might just lead you to a more ingenious, original path forward.

WHAT DOES THIS LOOK LIKE IN REAL LIFE?

Let's say you're stuck in traffic, and you default to the Pressured Way. Your eyes are bouncing between the clock and the car in front of you, and you're compulsively refreshing the GPS and growing increasingly agitated, leaning on your horn, wishing you had taken a different route. If you take the Playful Way, you accept that you're at a standstill, turn up the radio, and sing along, releasing stress as you do so. You get attentive and notice the other drivers, the graffiti on the highway divider, the clouds in the sky and the shapes they're making.

In scenario one, you are resistant to what's happening, fighting what is out of your control, and ultimately growing more tense. In scenario two, you are accepting the situation and finding a way to make it more enjoyable. Nothing measurably changed the situation—neither approach helped you "solve" the traffic—but each approach has a different effect on *you*. Which approach would be more stressful? Which would be more expansive?

With the Playful Way you're working *with* the challenge instead of *against* it. Especially when the challenge initially seems to be another person, this can be a refreshing approach. None of us wants to be stuck in a power struggle with our loved ones or colleagues. What if we invited people to play with us, rather than remaining locked in battle until one of us cries uncle?

THE PLAY SHIFT

When stress hijacks your brain, play can feel impossible. Your threat response wants you to fight, freeze, or flee, not get curious and creative. So, it takes getting used to doing things differently.

Here's a four-step process that I use to shift gears from reactive to resourceful. I call it the PLAY Shift—it's a combo of techniques I picked up in therapy (and from my behavioral therapist mom), melded with improv.

The PLAY Shift

When you find yourself getting rigid or reactive, try running through these steps.

P—Pause and Notice

What's happening in your body and mind right now?
- Feel your feet on the ground
- Name what you're reacting to

- Notice where you're feeling tension
- Note what emotions you're feeling

L—Lighten

Release some of that stress physically. It'll help you emotionally too.
- Take three deep, slow belly breaths
- Shake out your limbs, dance, or stretch
- Put your hand on your heart
- Hum, sing, or laugh (even forced laughter releases endorphins)

A—Accept what's happening

You don't have to like it, but fighting what's outside your control drains energy.
- Tell yourself, "This is happening whether I like it or not"
- Identify what's changeable and what's not
- Release the urge to control the uncontrollable
- Say, "I feel pressure but I choose playful"

Y—"Yes, and" I am Playful

Now tap into your play powers to work with the situation.
- Once you've paused, lightened, and accepted what's happening, you can choose to respond as your most creative, flexible self.
- Ask "What would my most playful self do here?"
- Wonder "If this were a game, what would my next move be?"
- Consider "How can I work with this situation instead of fighting it?"

The beauty of "Yes, and" thinking is that it doesn't require you to pretend everything is wonderful. It simply asks: "Given that this is happening, how might I work with it rather than against it?"

Quick example: Your partner says you've been on your phone too much lately. Instead of getting defensive, you **pause** to notice that you're bristling and your partner looks hurt. You **lighten** by taking a deep breath and unclenching your jaw. You **accept** their perspective as valid, acknowledging: "I have been distracted lately." You say "**Yes, and . . .**" "I have been buried in my phone." "Let's lock our devices in a drawer tonight and have a dance party."

The PLAY Shift helps us give space to our emotions, reminds us to shake off stress, to move from resistance to acceptance, and, in doing so, be ready to find solutions.

IMPERFECTLY PLAYFUL

I'll be honest: sometimes the Playful Way feels impossible. It's totally natural to resist new approaches when you're already stressed—our brains are wired to stick with familiar patterns, even when they're not working. When you're overwhelmed or dealing with a super difficult situation, "just be playful" can sound like extra pressure or toxic positivity.

I experienced this during my daughter's bedtime when someone in the next building over started blasting music at a decibel level so loud that it set off the "dangerously high" noise alert on my smartwatch. After twenty minutes, I was fuming: "Don't they know it's kids' bedtimes right now?!" I jumped into the neighbor group chat, where everyone was in the same "What the hell?!" state, further provoking each other's frustration.

Recognizing I was spiraling into the Pressured Way, I tried to shift: I **paused** to acknowledge my anger and spiked blood pressure. **Lightened** with deep breaths. **Accepted** that this was happening and that I couldn't control the noise level. But when I tried to find a playful **"Yes, and"** solution . . . nothing clever came. My daughter and I simply hid under blankets to dampen the noise until it finally stopped an hour later.

I hadn't come up with a playful solution, but the process still helped us to get a little calmer—and that's a win. The next time they blasted the music, I knew I didn't want to repeat the stress spiral, and this time I knew what my "Yes, and" solution was: my daughter and I chose to dance, pretending we were the ones throwing the party.

Here's the thing: play is a great tool to add to our toolkit and can be useful in many situations, but it isn't going to be the right fit for every task.

Life is messy and it's not always easy to embrace a brilliant playful solution in the midst of mayhem. But if you even try it, if you even *consider* it, that's major. Being open to the *possibility* of play as a solution is a giant step.

None of this is about perfection; it's about practice. Sometimes you'll move through all four steps with ease, and sometimes you'll only manage the first two or three. That's okay. Every attempt and partial success builds you up for the next challenge.

ROOTED BENDING

Sometimes we resist flexibility because we fear it means abandoning our values or letting people walk all over us. We've somehow convinced ourselves that being adaptable means being a pushover.

But that's like saying a tree can't have both roots in the ground and leaves that dance in the wind. You can defend what's most important to you while accepting a challenge and considering someone else's needs too.

The Playful Way offers something delightfully subversive: What if the strongest position isn't standing rigid like a statue but swaying like a groovy little reed? What if power isn't about controlling circumstances but skillfully collaborating with them?

Think of it as "rooted bending": staying anchored in your core values while flexibly adapting your approach. It's about knowing what's truly nonnegotiable for you (your roots) and what's adaptable (your branches).

When you feel yourself resisting change or grasping for control, ask yourself

- What core values am I trying to protect?
- What aspect of this situation is truly nonnegotiable for me?
- Where might I have flexibility?
- What becomes possible if I bend?

A HUNDRED WAYS TO BRUSH YOUR TEETH

This concept of rooted bending has really come in handy in the nightly battle of teeth brushing with my daughter, Viva. This mundane task has become the perfect laboratory for practicing (and sometimes failing spectacularly at) the Playful Way.

Initially, when Viva started refusing to brush her teeth, I'd flush with anger, thinking, "Why is she defying me?!" I'd say, "Come on, V. Just brush your teeth!" I made the process more pressured by trying to cajole, force, and display my disappointment. Many nights turned into a standoff that ended with tears on her side and guilt on mine.

What was happening? I was taking the Pressured Way and treating the how of toothbrushing as if it were not adaptable. But when I stepped back, I realized the only true nonnegotiable was dental health—the teeth needed to get brushed—but how we did it could be flexible.

So, I took a beat and returned with the Playful Way. I announced, "I'm not going to brush your teeth tonight. Mona, the bunny, told me she really wants to try it today!" I held her stuffed animal aloft. Viva broke into a grin.

The novelty and humor of it won her over. I had fun with it, doing a silly voice for the stuffed bunny, making carrot jokes, and high-fiving Viva with Mona's paw at the end. I walked away relieved and happy. No tears and clean teeth!

The bunny approach worked for a week. After that, I had to keep improvising and coming up with different ways to keep toothbrushing exciting. For a while, I played different dentist characters with elaborate backstories. We did competitions, lining up her own toys as "prizes" for brushing. Then we had a phase of musical toothbrushing where I'd make different notes and noises for each section of her teeth that she brushed. For a few weeks after my daughter's ballet recital, we did the "Dance of the Seven Toothbrushes," pirouetting and plié-ing as she brushed, accompanied by Tchaikovsky.

This might sound like a big ordeal. I sometimes wither with the amount of effort toothbrushing takes and wish I had a compliant child who obediently brushed her teeth with no pushback. But I have accepted that I don't have such a child. Sometimes I think (as others have told me) that I made toothbrushing "too much fun" and that now games are the only way to get it done (you made your bed!). Then I check myself, remembering that the Pressured Way always felt horrible.

The Playful Way hasn't made my life easier here, per se. But it has made me laugh more, helped me connect with my kid, and given me some very amusing stories to tell. I maintain firm roots (the teeth must be brushed) while allowing the leaves to sway flexibly with whatever way the wind is blowing that day.

There are often no easy options in life, but I'll take the creative labor of choosing the Playful Way over the emotional toil and stress of pushing through the Pressured Way any day.

FLUID OVER FIXED

One of the trickiest challenges to roll with? Other people's limited imagination of who we can be. As a fluid, bisexual person, I have often butted up against narrow guardrails of who other people think I am allowed to be. People have wanted to stuff me in one neat box and have fought to wrestle me into that constricted definition. At times I let them have power over me—let them tell me I "don't count," that my identity "was a phase," that I'm "greedy" to have a multiplicity of desires. The gray zone makes most people incredibly uncomfy.

You don't have to be queer to know this feeling. Maybe you're the creative one in a family of engineers, forever fielding questions about when you'll get a "real job." Maybe you're the ambitious woman who's been told she's "too much." Maybe you contain contradictions that make other people nervous—gentle *and* fierce, analytical *and* dreamy. Maybe you've shape-shifted through life and people keep wanting to pin you to who you were at twenty-two.

Other people wanting your identity to be fixed and definable is a trap. And it's one we can choose to slip out of.

When I choose the Playful Way, I choose to flow with my sweeping, fluid spirit: the one that says I can be everything at once—full, complex, multifaceted, expansive. The more I embrace it, the more permission I give those around me to embrace their own complexity too.

When someone challenges our identity, we can respond playfully: *improvisationally*, by "yes, and"-ing ourselves instead of defending; *curiously*, by wondering why they need us to be smaller; *experimentally*, by treating who we are as a living question rather than a fixed thing to protect.

The playful spirit wiggles out of boxes. It refuses the either/or and chooses the both/and. When we choose the Playful Way, we remember that who we are was never meant to be a final answer but an ongoing, improvisational act.

* * *

When faced with a challenge, our first reaction can be to resist. We see the obstacle as a nuisance, something we have to roll up our sleeves and grit our teeth for and *puuuush* out of our way. But approaching challenges this way can be draining, stressful, and a missed opportunity to discover what the obstacle might offer us in return.

When we approach a challenge playfully, we see the obstacle as a curiosity, something to inspect, to explore, to climb on top of and get a different view. We believe that there could be something to learn from this boulder that got dropped in our path, imagining that, perhaps, the way around it has a hidden surprise or benefit.

The Playful Way may help you reach your goals in new ways. But more important, it changes how you experience change and challenges. It helps you be the reed that bends with the wind instead of the oak that breaks. When things shift (and they always do), you're already moving. You adapt. You roll with it. You skip along lightly.

Your "Practice the Playful Way" Toolkit
Develop Your Adventurous Improviser Powers

The Flash Recap: Change happens, whether we like it or not, and our first instinct is usually to resist and control (aka the Pressured Way). But fighting reality wastes energy we could be using for creative problem-solving. Adventurous Improvisers know that flexibility beats rigidity—by saying "Yes, and" to life's curveballs, we find solutions and enjoy the journey, the Playful Way.

Wiggle Room: Whenever a small disruption occurs (like traffic, a canceled plan, or unexpected rain), pause and observe whether you're going the Pressured Way or the Playful Way in how you react.

Play Practice
Play Dates

An invitation to adventure and improvisation

Plan loose adventures that invite you to say "Yes, and" to unexpected discoveries. Have a starting point but stay open to detours and whims.

How to Practice

1. Schedule one or two adventures per month (either solo or with others).
2. Have a starting point but welcome unexpected detours and follow whims.
3. Collect stories and remember that mishaps can make for great memories.
4. Notice when you want to stick to the plan, then practice flexibility instead.

Adventure Possibilities

- **Neighborhood Exploration:** Pick an area to poke around and wind your way through
- **Museum Wander:** Visit with no agenda other than to find things that surprise you
- **Foodie Adventure:** Set out in search of a special food or let the server pick for you
- **Local Discovery:** Ask a local to direct you to their favorite hidden gem nearby
- **Shop Hop:** Explore the grocery store aisles in search of surprises

The goal isn't to have perfect plans but to roll with what comes your way. Like a good improviser, approach each play date with the willingness to say "Yes, and" to life's unexpected offers. The most memorable adventures often begin when we let go of controlling the outcome and embrace the joy of discovery.

In mundane moments
a glimmer hides

Within errands, routines,
there it resides

Each boring task can be remixed

With games and whimsy
in our bag of tricks

What if we saw with fresh delight

The sparkle in an ordinary sight?

CHAPTER 4

Strike Gold in Boredom

Jazz Up the Mundane Through Reframes and Games

> You can do it like it's a great weight on you, or you can do it like it's part of the dance.
>
> *Ram Dass*

Strike Gold in Boredom

In the 1964 classic film Mary Poppins, the magical nanny—dressed in her fitted white apron and little red bow tie—sings to the children as she cheerfully cleans up the house. She presents cleaning as a game and soon they're all happily participating, magically snapping their fingers, sending toys flying into chests, clothes sailing into drawers, and comforters unrolling onto beds.

We may not have Mary's supernatural powers, but we all possess something equally powerful: the ability to revamp our everyday moments through play. The Mundane Alchemist within us can turn boring routines into gold through the magic of games and reframes.

Even if we don't always feel like whistling as we fold towering mounds of laundry, run errands, or tick off to-dos at work, discovering our own tricks can help us find more enjoyment and engagement in our daily duties. If we're choking down our tasks like bitter black coffee, we can sweeten things up by sprinkling a spoonful of play into our daily lives.

This is the essence of what playful people do. They don't just endure daily routines; they remix and enliven them. They recognize that the ordinary moments make up the vast majority of our lives, and by approaching these moments with an imaginative seasoning, they can brew daily delight rather than merely waiting for special occasions to savor.

When my daughter refuses to take a bath, I offer up alternatives. Would you like to have a pool party? (A bath with a pool float in it and upbeat music.) Take a speed bath? (A timed bathing race.) Or enjoy a spa bath? (Add relaxing tunes and a candle.) Poof! A must-do has been sprinkled with sugar and now it's a want-to-do that feels lighter for us both.

Life happens in the spaces between the highlights (the commutes, the chores, the waiting rooms, the routines), and with some Mundane Alchemist magic, we can gussy them up and make them come alive.

THE MYSTERY TOUR EFFECT

My friend Dev Aujla's dad was a reframing genius, though Dev didn't discover this until he was an adult looking back on his childhood.

When Dev was growing up, he and his brother spent the weekends with their father while his mom worked hospital shifts as a nurse. These weren't ordinary father-son weekends; they were legendary adventures that Dev and his brother eagerly awaited all week. On Saturday morning, their dad would announce they were going on a Mystery Tour.

"We never knew where we were going," Dev explained of the adventures, "but there would always be unexpected twists."

His dad would drive to puzzling locations in the middle of nowhere and then challenge the boys, at ages six and eight, to navigate their way home. They would call out directions while their dad followed their commands. When they inevitably got lost, his father would switch up the game. They'd pick a car and follow it for as long as possible, pretending to be spies trailing their target while trying not to be detected.

Dev's father installed a button labeled "hyperdrive" that the boys could press in crucial moments. They swear they heard the engine rev and felt the car suddenly accelerate with supernatural power.

These Mystery Tours became the stuff of family lore—escapades so thrilling it took Dev thirty years to see what was actually going on. "I realized that we were doing things my dad had to do anyway," Dev reflected. The enigmatic Mystery Tours? They were just a magical reframing of regular weekend errands. The peculiar destinations were routine stops: the hardware store, the garbage dump, a lighting shop. The car the spy crew was tailing just happened to be going in the right direction home. The hyperdrive button came from a novelty shop, attached with tape.

Dev's dad dressed obligation up in a sparkly cape, turning regular old chores into a fantastical game. Why run errands when you can take your superhero vehicle on a top-secret mission instead?

FROM WORK TO PLORK

Artist and educator Corita Kent coined the term "plork" to describe the flow state when work and play effortlessly become one. I love this hilarious word and have adopted it as a reminder that I can choose to make my daily work more playful.

My cofounder Lakshmi and I are always asking ourselves how we can turn our work into plork as we build our creative play company NoomaLooma. For us, that means intentionally sprinkling delight onto the droll. We'll fill spreadsheet cells with bright colors, add emojis to our app's bug tracker (the ladybug is in heavy rotation, naturally), give our meetings ridiculous names, and send each other songs to go with dreaded tasks ("Here's a cinematic score to make filling out expenses feel like a hero's journey."). Best of all, plorking doesn't need to add time or difficulty to the tasks at hand. I still wish I didn't have to look at legal docs but, since I do, I might as well pair it with fun music or give the time block on my calendar a silly name.

Check out the vibe shift on these routines:

- Chore: "I need to clean the kitchen" → Plork: "I'm going to take a 'before' picture, set a fifteen-minute timer, and see how much better I can get the 'after' image to be by the time I'm done"

- Inbox Triage: "47 unread messages" → Plork: "I'm putting on a cinematic score and clearing emails like a hero"
- Meeting: "Another weekly update" → Plork: "Corporate buzzword bingo begins now"

These small shifts don't change the task itself, but they do create wiggle room in our relationship to it. Space where we lighten the load a bit and maybe even surprise ourselves by getting into a playful flow with it.

Recently, while hosting a play workshop, I asked the group what chore they hated most. The unanimous answer was laundry. We did a quick three-minute brainstorm on how we could bring more play to this dreaded task. Here are some ideas the group came up with:

- Play bingo with socks
- Put on music and make a shirt your dance partner
- Invent stories about the next adventure the clothes will go on
- Fold clothes into unexpected new outfits
- FaceTime a friend and have a live laundry folding race

Making this list made everyone smile. Even if we don't try these exact ideas, a sense of possibility starts to appear just by imagining them. Maybe laundry or filing expense reports will never be truly fun . . . but it could certainly be made funner with a pop of play.

THE GOLD MINE OF BOREDOM

You're standing in line at the post office. The person at the counter is asking about every possible shipping option to Antarctica. That familiar itch of boredom creeps in. Do you:

a. Pull out your phone and start scrolling through social media
b. Start imagining elaborate backstories for why someone needs to urgently ship something to Antarctica
c. Strike up a conversation with the equally bored person behind you
d. Invent a mental game where you find objects in alphabetical order around the room

If you picked A, congratulations—you're human in our digital age! We've become so used to filling every spare moment with our phones that the very idea of empty time makes us twitchy. That slim rectangle in our pocket is like an escape hatch for boredom, ready to beam us away from the present at any hint of an awkward or quiet moment. But what if these dull moments aren't dead time to escape but open space waiting for your playful spirit to create?

A 2019 study in the *Academy of Management Discoveries* found that periods of boredom followed by unstructured time led to significantly more original solutions to problems than continuous stimulation. Boredom nudges our brains toward creative thinking that our brains want to search for through divergent thinking and exploration. Think of boredom as your brain's way of saying, "Hey, let's make something interesting happen!"

Illustrator and author Maira Kalman describes her creative process as "the discipline of looking at what is in front of you when nothing is in front of you." Boredom is the blank canvas from which you can create something new. When we resist the urge to scroll away these moments, we allow space for a flow of fresh ideas.

That's exactly what Mundane Alchemists do—they find fascination in emptiness. They craft narratives about a distant lover, stationed in Antarctica, getting hot cocoa in the mail, invent mental games unlocking points with each advance in line, and count all the colorful things brightening a drab post office.

GAME ON: TURNING TASKS INTO CHALLENGES

A dash of competition can turn even the most tedious moments into surprisingly engaging challenges.

During a recent ferry commute, my daughter begged me to let her fill her boredom by playing a game on my phone, wailing, "I'm soooo bored!" Instead, I quickly scanned the space around us and invented an impromptu word game using the snack bar packaging. "We have to come up with words using the letters on the snack wrappers," I explained. "Each player gets one point per letter used, and the person with the most points wins!"

She spelled "door" using letters from the Doritos bag. I put together "pity" using letters from "Pocky" and "Doritos." She found "cheer" in "Cheetos" and "Oreos." The game continued for ten rounds as she kept score, eventually winning. I felt triumphant for turning a bored moment into screen-free family fun that also doubled as spelling and math practice.

The beauty of gamification lies in its versatility and simplicity. You might set a timer and race to beat your personal best for getting your expense report done, devise a points system for daily tasks, or play word games with the ads you see during commutes.

This works wonders because our brains respond powerfully to goals, challenges, and rewards. Neuroscience research has shown that when we engage in gamelike activities, our brains release dopamine—the same "feel-good" neurotransmitter associated with pleasure and motivation. We're basically tricking our reward-seeking brains into getting excited about boring stuff.

I've been a natural game-maker my whole life. Stuck in long

Catholic masses as a kid, I devised an elaborate mental milestone system: making it to the first hymn, then the reading, counting down to communion. As an adult, I still use that trick when I'm running. Instead of focusing on the whole distance (overwhelming!), I count smaller victories: making it to the lamp post, getting to the park entrance, and hitting the halfway point. When I'm writing, I use a star chart system to visualize milestones: for every one thousand words I earn a star and enjoy the deep satisfaction of coloring it in.

The rules are simple: outline clear goals, add a scoring system, and establish rewards or consequences (or simple cheering). Whether you're folding a mountain of laundry or sitting through an insufferable status meeting, adding game elements can shift the experience from obligation to opportunity.

LIFE: THE MUSICAL!

A simple soundtrack change can give main character energy and turn a routine task into a silver screen—worthy scene, adding music, narration, or a dash of dramatic flair to everyday moments.

Think about it: A run to UPS would feel entirely different when accompanied by upbeat soca music versus melancholic piano. A routine grocery run evolves into a Parisian adventure with French pop ballads in your headphones. The soundtrack you choose rewrites the story of your day.

When Anjelika Temple's family needs to clean the house and inevitably no one wants to, she shouts, "It's time for a DANCE PARTY CLEAN-UP!" Each member of the family chooses an upbeat track to get the job done. Dancing with the mops and brooms is highly encouraged, as is shaking their booties while they work. They channel silliness and evoke giggles as they spruce up their home.

When he had chores to do growing up, Dan Saks's older brother would say: "Come on, we'll put on music. It'll be fun!" This simple phrase worked wonders in inspiring him to action and is an encouragement he now uses with his own kids when there's laundry to be folded or mess to be tidied. To-dos become an opportunity for shared activity together, a fun soundtrack whisking the broom and the time along.

As a new mom, Liz Tran reinvented her routines by composing custom songs for her regular duties. As she diapers her baby, she sings a catchy tune: "I wanna know what's up with you, I wanna know if you did number two . . ." She has songs for bedtime, diaper changes, and dishes—turning repetitive tasks into musical moments that make both her and her baby smile. "These little songs make me laugh," she says, "and they seem to entertain the baby too, which makes the daily rituals feel fresh each time."

These simple musical additions can reinvigorate how we approach routine tasks. By changing the soundtrack, we make space in the day-to-day for role-play, daydreaming, and glee.

When faced with a pile of dishes or a stack of paperwork, ask yourself: What would the soundtrack be if this moment were in a movie? Are you in an action sequence, a romantic montage, or perhaps the triumphant climax where the hero finally conquers the laundry mountain?

EVERYDAY MAGICIANS IN OUR MIDST

They're all around us—the Mundane Alchemists who can make the routine moments of our day come alive. Maybe it's your coworker who gives every meeting a silly nickname ("Not Another Tuesday" or "The Great Spreadsheet Summit of 2025"), or the deli owner who asks you a trivia question every time you stop in for a coffee. They're the people who enhance routine interactions with moments of connection and delight.

In my own neighborhood, I've discovered many of these everyday magicians:

Jose Duyanda, a doorman in my apartment building, does polls with the tenants. He'll greet us in the lobby with questions like "If you could have any superpower, what would it be?," kicking off conversations and friendly debates among neighbors. Sitting at the front desk is often tedious during his eight-hour shift, so his polls entertain him. He makes them a game for himself, guessing what people he's interacted with for years will answer. Sometimes he's right and sometimes he's surprised, with new insights into the people he sees every day.

Another doorman, Sammy Bajraktarevi, sings morning greetings operatically—"Happppyyy Mondayyyy"—while sweeping his arms up in the air with theatrical flair.

The crossing guard, Lucy, always smiles and waves, and stops to chat with people in the neighborhood, eliciting smiles when she holds out her fists and says, "Pick a hand," then reveals a lollipop to the lucky kids who choose correctly.

Felix Taxeras, a building superintendent, leaves gold chocolate coins outside our apartment doors and then tells us he saw a leprechaun running through the hallway.

These people instinctually find ways to make their day-to-day more engaging, lighthearted, and fun, even with repetitive tasks. Their approaches also generate shared moments with those around them through micro interactions, creating a more connected community at large. These are the people who bring the color and warmth to the neighborhoods we live in, making it home.

They sprinkle a bit of whimsy into our daily routines, unearthing joy in everyday moments, often without even realizing the ripple effects of their small acts of magic.

Your "Strike Gold in Boredom" Toolkit
Develop Your Mundane Alchemist Powers

The Flash Recap: The ability to reimagine ordinary moments into extraordinary ones isn't magic—it's a mindset. By approaching routine tasks with curiosity and fresh thinking, we discover spaces for joy and surprise in unexpected places.

Wiggle Room: As you're waiting in line or have a moment of in-between time, see if you can resist the urge to look at your phone and look around instead.

Play Practice
Routine Remix

Turn boring tasks into micro adventures

Jazz up your most tired tasks into something you might actually look forward to. This practice is about adding tiny twists that take routines from "ughh" to "kinda fun."

How to Practice

1. Pick one routine task that usually elicits an internal eye roll.
2. Add one playful twist to make it more engaging.
3. Try your remix and see how it changes your energy and relationship to the task.

4. Repeat successful remixes and dream up new ones for your repertoire.

Ways to Remix

- **Challenges:** Set timers for speed, create personal bests to beat, invent elaborate scoring systems, or make silly awards ("Fastest Dishwasher in the West").
- **Atmosphere Shifts:** Change the lighting, add scents, or transform the environment (welcome to my disco kitchen).
- **Musical:** Add a soundtrack that changes the whole vibe—upbeat for energy, classical for elegance, or something silly for giggle factor.
- **Adventure Framing:** Turn errands into mystery tours and commutes into scavenger hunts.
- **Playful Naming:** Give the task a rebrand by presenting it with a fancy new name. (It's not a financial review; it's a Budget Bonanza.)

Try whatever appeals to your sense of play or sounds amusing. Some remixes will stick, others won't—that's the point of experimenting. Not every moment will sparkle, but you may discover how small playful additions can revamp your relationship with necessary tasks and add a little gold dust to your day.

We think it's best when
times are tough

To avoid the heavy, scary stuff

But even when the day is dark

We can light it with a playful spark

Explore the shadows, find new ways

Create substance from
the toughest days

CHAPTER 5

Play with Shadows

Find your way through challenging times with creative expression as a compass

Maybe it was the willingness to play that hinted at a tender, eternally newborn part in all humans. Maybe it was the willingness to play that kept one from despair.

Gabrielle Zevin

Play with Shadows

Trigger warning: this chapter includes mentions of miscarriage and sexual assault.

We tend to think of play as being easy breezy, but it allows for an exploration of our darkest sides and deepest fears. When kids play, it's not all rainbows and unicorns. Oftentimes, they are getting into some freaky territory. They shoot at each other with finger guns, set up an orphanage for their dolls, or draw the house engulfed in flames. In their playful exploration, there's room for children to delve into their fears. This is a huge part of how kids process the difficult and overwhelming elements of life.

As adults, we tend to meet serious problems with serious energy and to try to think and talk our way through fears. When experiencing painful emotions, we often close up to protect ourselves. However, in these difficult moments, playfulness can be a gentle tool to help us stay open and connected to ourselves, and our support systems.

When we embrace things with the spirit of Expressive Creators, whether through writing, music, storytelling, or visual design, we give ourselves permission to explore our problems rather than be frozen by them.

Often, we can't change the fact that things are dark. Tragedies happen, losses occur, hope can appear futile. But it is possible to play in that darkness. When the lights are out, we may have to be more careful so we don't hurt ourselves. We might encounter distress. But just as our eyes adjust to see in the dark, our hearts and minds can adapt to find lightness in heavy situations.

That's what happens when we bring our artistic spirit to life's hardest moments. Instead of hiding from difficult emotions or experiences, we can learn to explore them with curiosity and creativity.

THE STORIES WE TELL IN THE DARK

The stories we tell ourselves about our fears matter more than we think.

Imagine you're in a dark room and see a tall, daunting figure. Your mind spins a story: this is a dangerous intruder coming to get you. But you pause, take a deep breath, and look closer. Rather than pull the covers over your head, you blink a few times to let your vision adapt. Peering into the darkness, you discover that the "intruder" is just the elongated shadow of a coatrack—nothing more than an innocent piece of furniture holding your outerwear.

Like a harmless shadow morphing into a menace in our minds, our fears can often loom larger in the darkness of our thoughts. Playing with shadows helps us look closer, engage our curiosity, and see things from new perspectives. What seemed terrifying might reveal itself as manageable (or even comical!), and if things are genuinely as scary as we fear, we can gain new insights by exploring rather than hiding.

And when you share that story with a friend, how terrified you were of the "intruder" that turned out to be a winter coat, the shared laughter and relief strengthens your bond. Similarly, playing together in dark times—whether it's using gallows humor, giving your fear a silly code name, or sharing your story—can foster connection and mutual support.

By playing with shadows, we're not denying the existence of our coatrack "intruders." Instead, we use creativity to engage with shadows, transforming our relationship with the unknown and the feared, and with each other. It reminds us that even in our darkest moments, we have the capacity to create light through play, laughter, and human connection.

Of course, not all difficulties can be reduced to a coatrack shadow—pain is real, and some experiences are genuinely devastating. Playing with shadows isn't about minimizing suffering or forcing positivity; it's about finding a way to engage with difficult realities on your own terms, when you're ready.

HIDE-AND-SEEK IN THE FOREST OF GRIEF

For years, I had been playing a game of hide-and-seek with motherhood, searching for it through a maze of health issues and medical procedures. Along the way, I discovered I had hypothyroidism, PCOS, fibroids, and what I thought a lab tech said was a "unicorn uterus" (how magical!) but was actually a half uterus, aka a "unicornuate uterus" (a lot smaller and less sparkly). Each diagnosis sent me around another bend.

Then, one summer, I thought I'd finally found it. Multiple sonograms confirmed I was pregnant and the baby was healthy. I was past my first trimester, walking to work on a sunny day, with a visible bump and a hopeful bounce in my step. All was good.

A few hours later, as a big meeting ended, I stood up to leave the conference room and sensed a sudden rush. The world around me blurred, my heart raced, and I started walking quickly toward the bathroom, trying to mask my panic. It wasn't until I was in the office bathroom stall that I dared to look down. My pants were soaked in blood and there were splatters on my glittery silver sandals.

At 1 a.m., after almost seven hours in the ER, the doctors came into my hospital room to tell me my baby's heart was no longer beating.

Miscarriage is a mind fuck on so many levels. For me, all jumbled together were the horror show of bleeding profusely in the office bathroom; the exhaustion of a many-years-long pregnancy journey now reset to zero; shame about my body's "failure" (and feminist shame about that shame); grief for someone I had never met but dreamed a big life for; and the harsh recalibration of my hopes for motherhood.

It's amazing how much you can love and grieve a person you've never met. It's a lonely sensation. Especially because, in contrast, you know how surrounded with community you would be if you'd given birth. You'd also be surrounded by community if you'd lost a person who existed in the external world—you'd get together, have a service, share memories; you'd have a ritual for grieving.

I quickly realized that there was no common protocol, no recognized ritual for miscarriage in my culture—and that I was going to have to make my own meaning, follow my intuition, and with imagination and creativity forge a path to recovery for myself. I decided to go into the darkness and play with my grief.

First, journaling became my flashlight, illuminating the dark corners of my emotions. I poured out unfiltered thoughts, play-by-play recaps of what happened, and thoughts I couldn't voice aloud. This act of documentation became a form of play, a way to understand my pain rather than run from it.

Then, my partner and I sat down to write a letter to our vanished child. It was a tearful bonding act that helped us express as a couple what we had lost. We were playing make-believe, addressing a child we would never know, saying goodbye to her and to the life we had dreamed up. Writing our own epilogue of sorts. This imaginary correspondence became a way of giving our grief shape.

One night, I woke up at 3:30 a.m. and started writing. A poem spilled out, surprising me with its raw honesty. I hadn't written poetry since eighth grade, but here I was, playing with words in the darkest hours of the night. I decided to share the poem on Instagram, turning my private play public. Hearing and reading the dozens of replies to my story made me less isolated. Opening up became a conduit to connection, to find others who were also stumbling through the forest of grief.

But the heaviness persisted, and I often found myself holding my breath, trying to prevent emotions from coming. Then my friend invited me to karaoke. She was waiting for a breast cancer diagnosis and wanted to get her mind off things. While I normally love karaoke, it was the last activity I wanted to engage in. But I wanted to be a good friend, so I went.

At karaoke, I let go. I wailed. I screamed, moved, and expressed. We sang angsty '90s songs and anthems to surviving heartbreak, like Whitney Houston's "I Will Always Love You." It was the antidote to holding my breath.

This loud, raucous play became a release valve for my grief. It was as if we were playing tag with our emotions, chasing them down with each song, touching them briefly before running away again. There was humor to the song selection, leaning into the camp of singing my heartbreak. As I belted out "Shattered Dreams" by Johnny Hates Jazz, I had to laugh.

As I continued trying to understand and acknowledge my evolving grief, I explored different modes of expression. I started adding songs to a Heartbreak Playlist: each tune or lyric was a potential hiding place for an aspect of my grief. Other days I found myself in the kitchen, chopping vegetables with all of my might, pouring love into a soup pot, letting the rhythmic actions and familiar scents ground me in the present moment.

In the end, I got my "happy ending" with the birth of my

daughter, Viva, but as they say, "grief doesn't go away, life just grows around it." The experience taught me that play doesn't always mean joy or laughter; sometimes it means creative engagement with our grief, a way to befriend it rather than hide from it. We can use our imagination to create conversations that never got to happen, our voices to express pain and share our stories, our bodies to release tension and be in community with one another.

When we play with shadows, we don't diminish our pain. We honor it, we explore it, and ultimately, we find our way through it.

FINDING EACH OTHER THROUGH STORIES

Later, a piece I wrote to process my grief made its way to author and storyteller Georgia Clark, who asked me to tell my story onstage at her intergenerational storytelling show, Generation Women. I'd be joined by a group of women and nonbinary performers ranging from their twenties to their nineties, all with a personal story to share.

I was still stewing in the shame of miscarriage, and the conventional wisdom would have been to keep it private, to process it quietly. I had learned there was another path, the Playful Way, that involved bringing my story into the light, burning off the shame, and transmuting it into something that could connect with others. So I said yes to the stage.

The show starts with the youngest storyteller and goes from there, so I was second to perform and sat taking conscious deep breaths as the adrenaline coursed through my veins. The storyteller in her twenties was a comedian and I was grateful to have a few laughs to relieve my anxiety.

My turn arrived and I stepped into the spotlight; the audience vignetted and went quiet. My voice caught in my throat, but I took a breath and pushed the words out. I explored what had happened to me out loud, lifting the lid on my bubbling pot of emotions, revealing the hurtful things people had said to me. As the audience touched their hearts in empathy, faces wide open with concern, and laughed at absurd moments, a sense of power emerged. This unwanted, unexpected thing had happened to me, but I was still here commanding the room with my story. I delivered my final lines and the room erupted in applause.

I plopped down in my seat relieved, elated. Then I was able to listen to the older women in the show share stories. As storytellers in their forties, fifties, sixties, and seventies told their tales of heartbreak, navigating difficult relationships, and grief, I dabbed tears from the corner of my eye, doubled over in fits of laughter, and nodded my head in understanding.

Science confirms what storytellers have always known: our brains are wired for narrative. Sharing our stories, especially the difficult ones, builds empathy and helps us make meaning from hard experiences.

I've now performed on the Generation Women stage many times—and as a result, in other storytelling shows as well—sharing stories of sorrow and hijinks, misadventures and mortal embarrassment. What always strikes me is how the best stories often come from experiences that are deeply painful or embarrassing in the moment. How when we get enough distance from our stories, we can tell them in a way that puts us in the driver's seat, moving our lives forward again.

Of course, telling a deeply personal story onstage is a tall order for most of us, especially if we're still processing. So I asked Georgia how she'd guide someone to explore their story in their own space and time.

She said the first thing is just to write it down: "Get the war out of your head and onto the page." Spill your guts onto the page, messy and unfiltered. Let the words tumble out in a big pile. If you're angry and need to vent, you could write it in the form of an email you'd never actually send (subject line: "Fuck you. Fuck you. FUCK YOU!") just to get out the raw emotion and move through it.

Another trick Georgia suggests (one she often practices as a modern romance writer) is to step outside ourselves, to slip into the skin of another. Write your story from a different perspective, she says. See how the light changes, how the shadows shift. We often forget that our experience is not universal, so trying to look at it from another vantage point can help us find a new way to interpret our story.

"There is an infinite amount of ways we can tell our own story," Georgia says. In telling our stories, we "reframe and reshape the events in our lives—particularly the hard ones—from failures into examples of resilience and grit." Psychologists call this "cognitive reframing."

When we reshape how we tell our stories, we literally rewire our brains. We shift from being passive characters to becoming the authors of our own lives. Every time someone steps up to that microphone, they're saying, "This happened to me, and here's how I'm choosing to understand it. Here's how I'm growing from it."

Sometimes, our stories cling to us, still tender and painful to the touch. Georgia reminds us—it's okay to wait. To let time work its alchemy. We often need space to find enough distance to look again, to rewrite the story, or even to laugh.

In the end, this is how we play with shadows: by telling our stories, by shaping them, reshaping them. By finding the courage to speak our truth and the wisdom to listen to others. We fumble in the darkness, hands outstretched, until we touch another's story. And in that touch, we find hope.

DRAWING BACK INTO LIFE

Chanel Miller, the powerful writer and artist who first became known to the world as "Emily Doe" in the Stanford sexual assault case, found an unexpected path toward healing through artistic expression. After her victim impact statement went viral and she later revealed her identity with her bestselling memoir *Know My Name*, Miller shared on the podcast *We Can Do Hard Things* how art became essential to her recovery.

Miller described how in the midst of navigating the grueling legal process and working on her memoir, her therapist offered an unusual suggestion: she wanted her to go to a trampoline park.

Her therapist told her to follow her pleasure as a part of her healing and urged her to do something playful and joyful. The adult gymnasium suggestion felt like a stretch, so Miller decided to do a "dialed-down version" and signed up for a narrative illustration class where she could learn to make comics.

Her days were consumed with writing her memoir, reliving difficult memories and examining painful experiences from her past. But evenings in her small class of seven people offered something different.

She started noticing things that were happening in her present life outside of the story she was telling about her past. She started to pay attention to the ways in which her life was still moving forward.

She translated moments from her day into simple drawings. One comic depicted her experience fostering senior dogs with incontinence issues. Living on a slanted hill in San Francisco meant that when the dogs would pee during the night, as they often did, it would trickle all the way across her room. In class, she documented these moments, using fluorescent highlighter to color the urine trails.

What might have seemed like mundanity or a nuisance was actually bringing her back to herself. Art was a way to get unstuck from the past and force her into living in the present. She began to pay attention to her life again.

These simple drawings grounded her in the present moment rather than keeping her trapped in trauma. She was able to notice how life continued to unfold around her despite everything she'd been through.

In crafting these small, often humorous observations of daily life, she was creating something entirely her own, something no court proceeding could define or diminish.

AN ALTAR FOR HARSH REALITIES

Sometimes reimagining the objects that represent our challenges can shift the story of what they mean to us. When my friend Lydia Pang was pregnant, she had to manage complex medical issues and found herself facing a daily regimen of brutal shots and pills.

At first, she hid the medicine in a cabinet. But each time she opened the door, a wave of shame washed over her—the cluttered collection of bottles and needles was a daily reminder of her illness, past losses, and lack.

Lydia is a creative director with a distinctively goth sense of style, and her home embodies her incredible design sense—each inch is immaculately arranged. So her wise mother suggested she redesign her medicine area to see if it might rearrange her feelings about it too. Lydia brought an antique table to sit near the vanity she uses when dressing up and doing her makeup. She crowned the table with a silver tray with sleek ceramics to hold her pills and syringes. She found a punk rock acid-green sharps container for needle disposal, added a candle and her favorite perfume, and even found a chic bottle of hand sanitizer. What previously looked sterile and scary now looked artful and ritualistic.

The medicine altar didn't take away the physical discomfort or evaporate all the anxiety, but it reimagined Lydia's relationship to it. By displaying rather than hiding these "ugly" necessities and surrounding them with beauty and intention, she reclaimed power over her experience and could approach it with less dread. The ritual became an act of creation rather than mere compliance, a daily practice of remaking the difficult into something with meaning and beauty.

Whether it's creating a still life, assembling an altar, or putting together an outfit that tells a story, expressive creation can take many forms, each powerful in its ability to shift how we view and relate to ourselves and our experiences.

A PATCHWORK OF LIVES

I stood in the living room of my childhood home and looked up at the patchwork quilt hanging on the wall. My gaze passed over the colorfully embroidered names, the appliquéd symbols—a saffron quilted sun, stitched sheet music, the shiny silver patch of a cross. The quilt—a small section of the NAMES Project AIDS Memorial Quilt—seemed to pulse with life, grief, and defiant love.

I was only eight, but I remember the energy in the air. Rather than things being somber, they were upbeat; our space was filled with unfamiliar faces and voices as people shared stories. My mom knelt beside me. "Each of these squares," she said, "represents someone who died from AIDS. Their families and friends made these to remember them."

I saw how the AIDS epidemic went beyond the news. It was real people with real stories. And their stories, like the patches made in their honor, were vibrant, textured, and beautiful.

Years later, I would come to understand the magnitude of the AIDS quilt project. How, in the face of a government that had turned its back, in the shadow of a society that often chose silence, people were making themselves heard with needle and thread. How it grew from a single panel in San Francisco to a massive tapestry of lives, too large to be displayed in its entirety. How it traveled the country, forcing America to confront the human cost of stigma and inaction.

Psychologists often talk about the importance of "meaning-making" in the face of loss. The quilt project gave people a tangible way to channel their grief into something productive and visible. The quilt also took one of the most insidious aspects of the AIDS crisis—how it isolated its victims—and shattered that by creating a network of shared experiences, an act of collective memory.

We can take the rawest materials of loss and create something that connects us, that moves us to action. Every stitch, every scrap of fabric chosen with care, is an act of love that echoes far beyond the hands that created it.

In a world that often wants us to look away from suffering, to keep our stories of grief and illness hidden, the quilt stands as a Technicolor shout: We were here. We loved. Our stories mattered.

* * *

Of course, playing with shadows takes many forms. Sometimes it's solemn and reverent, like crafting a quilt panel for a loved one.

Other times it might be finding unexpected beauty in trying circumstances, like Lydia's medicine altar.

Even the simplest stick figure drawing or words written just for yourself can shift something inside, regardless of how creative you believe you are.

If you're supporting someone in their darkness, resist the urge to fix or brighten. Offer them materials: a notebook, colored pencils, an invitation to wail together at karaoke. Sometimes the greatest gift is permission to express without pressure and let it be messy.

Whether we're writing through grief, singing our hearts out, or remodeling our spaces, artistic expression helps us find ways forward when logic alone can't guide us.

Your "Play with Shadows" Toolkit
Develop Your Expressive Creator Powers

The Flash Recap: When life is tough, our playful spirit can be a powerful compass. Through creative expression (whatever the medium), we rewrite our relationship with difficulty. By playing with shadows, we don't diminish our pain; we honor it while discovering new ways to move through it and remember we're not alone.

Wiggle Room: When experiencing a difficult emotion today, give it a color in your mind. Just this teensy act of imaginative acknowledgment can provide a tiny bit of breathing room between you and the feeling.

Play Practice
Flash Expressions

Quick creative bursts to shift your mood

When you're stuck, overwhelmed, or in need of perspective, this practice offers a simple way to express what's inside. "Small paper, short timeframe" means no perfection, just feelings spilling out.

How to Practice

1. Notice when you need an emotional release or perspective shift.
2. Grab any writing/drawing tool and a small piece of paper (index card, journal margin, Post-it).
3. Set a timer for two to five minutes (either mentally or physically).
4. Choose one expressive mode and let your hand move without judgment.
5. When finished, take a breath and notice any internal shifts.
6. Optional: Date it and keep a collection of these tiny snapshots.

Expressive Modes

- Brain Dump: Write two minutes of unfiltered thoughts, worries, or observations
- Mini Comic: Sketch a simple illustrative frame of the current situation (stick figures welcome!)
- Mood Music: Put on a song that reflects your mood and doodle along to the music

- Free Doodle: Make a scribble or abstract shape that matches your energy
- Note To Self: Write a note to yourself observing what's going on with you right now

Keep small paper scraps and a pen handy for your expressions. You don't need to create polished art to create clarity. These tiny bursts provide just enough space to acknowledge where you are without getting stuck there.

Our minds are so busy

Just buzzing with thoughts

So get in your body when
you're tied up in knots

That corporal zone where
our life force arose

Intuition, creativity,
connection just flows

Jump out of your head
and into the present

Dance around, you wild
little pheasant

CHAPTER 6

Move Out of Your Head

Get into your body to release anxiety and come alive

Dance first and think afterwards... it's the natural order.

Samuel Beckett

When do you feel most alive? I mean completely in the present moment, buzzing on another plane, in touch with all your senses, alive?

Maybe you're on the dance floor sensing the bass thrum through your chest, vibrating your very cells. Your arms sway of their own accord, feet tapping, light as air yet magnetically grounded to the beat. You catch the eye of someone, and instinctually, you're both swaying in sync, grinning and mirroring each other's gestures, rising up and down, side to side, twirling and bobbing, one living organism.

Or perhaps you're floating on your back in the ocean, yielding to the gentle rise and fall of the water. The sun warms your face while the cool water cradles you. Your ears dip just below the surface, revealing an otherworldly soundscape where your own heartbeat becomes audible along with the pops and crackles of air bubbles. The rhythm of your breath synchronizes with the swelling of the waves. Boundaries dissolve—where do you end and the water begin?

Or maybe you're running in the rain, each drop a splattering charge on your skin. Your feet slap against wet pavement, muscles stretching and contracting in a hum of motion. You're soaked to the bone and pulsing, connected to your physicality, *alive*.

We might not always realize it, but these moments of physical freedom are also quintessential play states where we're fully immersed, joyful, and present. So much of how we experience play throughout life is physical: through sports and dance and sex and the expressiveness with which we gesticulate, hands gliding through the air, as we tell a story.

The Movers and Shakers among us know best that our bodies are conduits for pure, unfiltered life force, reminding us of the release, joy, and exhilaration that comes from simply being in our physical forms.

BREAK FREE OF THE BLOB STATE

Sadly, this state of aliveness is a rarity for many of us. Much more of our time is spent with the scantest of motion, fingers tapping a keyboard (as I am now), finger swiping on a glass screen.

In that daily blob state, do you ever feel like you're just a head, your flesh and bones nothing more than a transportation device for your brain? You're not alone. In her book *The Wisdom of Your Body*, Hillary L. McBride, PhD, points out that in our modern Western world, we've become masters of the mind-body split. We're so caught up in our thoughts, notifications, and to-do lists that we've practically forgotten we have bodies at all (McBride 2021).

This floating-head existence cuts us off from ourselves. We lose touch with our physical selves, each other, and our sense of true aliveness when we try to exist only as brains.

Part of the problem is that we give WAYYYY too much credit to our thinking brains. We believe the myth that our minds hold the answer to everything related to intelligence, creativity, and emotions. That our physical instincts are lesser, maybe even dangerous, and should be restrained. But here's the paradox: by disconnecting from our bodies, we're actually sabotaging our brilliant brains. Turns out our bodies have a lot to say if we'd only listen.

Getting out of our heads and into our physical forms is a powerful way to connect with the essential elements of play—spontaneity, flow, and creative energy. It's a way to meet ourselves and each other on a different plane than regular old talk-talk-talking or think-think-thinking. In our pure physical states, insights and information bubble up from fresh, untapped wells.

Movement also helps us to let go of stress, which brings us to a more resourced state. We know this instinctively, and it's why we tell each other things like "Shake it off," "Go for a walk," "Sweat it out." Against our best instincts, though, we are often reluctant to prioritize getting physical, especially when we're busy, disconnected, and stressed out (i.e., when we need it most). We expect our brains to do all the heavy lifting, and we spiral into stress, getting tighter and tighter in our physical form. More blobbed out.

Before we go further, I want you to take a deep breath into your chest and then into your belly. Stop to notice as your abdomen expands with air. Hold your breath for a few seconds and see if you can detect your heart beating as you do. As you exhale, notice the air flowing out and your chest falling. Do a quick scan of the rest of your body. What sensations do you notice? Which parts are heavy? Which are light? Does anything hurt? Itch? Feel tight? Take a second; notice being in your physical self in this moment. If you did it, brownie points for you—you may now go forward. But first, shimmy your shoulders a little with me.

Now that we're feeling our flesh-and-bones selves, let's explore how physical expression can unlock our creativity, deepen our connections, and invite more joy into our lives.

WE'RE ALL WILD THINGS

When life gets tough or scary or overwhelming, what happens to your body? If you're like most of us humans living in our buttoned-up modern world, you probably freeze. You tense up. You hold your breath. Your shoulders creep up toward your ears. Your jaw clenches. And without realizing it, you stay that way.

It's fascinating to watch how differently wild animals handle stress. After enduring frightening or threatening events, animals instinctively know how to release the tension physically. A dog will shake vigorously, head to tail. A bird will repeatedly flap its wings with extra force. A gazelle will leap and bound after escaping danger. A vervet monkey will let out a specific vocalization that releases tension. Nature has programmed these physical releases into animals, and it's theorized that this is why wild creatures don't hold on to stress and trauma the way we humans do.

Here's what we forget: we're animals! We need a physical release of stress, too—but we've learned to override it. We zip it up, button it down, and push on. "Keep calm and carry on" might be the most physiologically harmful advice ever printed on a coffee mug.

Our bodies know more than we give them credit for. Research shows that when we engage with the world using our physical systems, we give our conscious minds a boost (Oppezzo 2014). Movement can help us access more insight than thinking alone. When we're caught in a thought loop of "I can't figure this out" or "I don't know what to do next," our physical selves may hold the keys to sensing, responding, and releasing in ways that can break us free from mental gridlock. We just need to listen and respond.

This applies to big emotions, too. Think about the last time you saw a child having a meltdown. They don't quietly suppress their feelings—they thrash, they cry, they stomp, they express the emotion through their bodies. And then, often in what seems like an impossibly quick transition, they're fine again, ready to play.

Somewhere along the way to adulthood, we silence this innate wisdom in pursuit of social harmony. We were taught to stay still, stay quiet, stay contained. Of course, this has its benefits. But by freezing up entirely, we may have lost our most natural pathway to equilibrium.

Once, amid one of my toddler's tantrums, I noticed myself growing tight and frustrated (and a little jealous of her uncontained wailing), so I started doing Lion's Breath, a simple breathwork technique. Sitting on the floor with my screaming toddler, I inhaled through my nose, then opened my mouth wide with my tongue sticking out and exhaled "haaaa" loudly while making claws with my hands. It was a release for the tension I was holding, and as I blew off stress, my daughter squealed with laughter. It was so funny to her that she forgot about her tantrum and wanted to join me in doing it over and over again.

The next time you feel like a pot of emotions ready to boil over, rather than just pushing the lid down, explore how you might let it out physically. What if you leaned into those animal instincts? Notice where tension lives in your physical self. Is your jaw clenched? Are your nails digging into your palms? Are your legs filled with jittery energy? Can you listen to your body's desire for release rather than zipping it up, even if it's in a tiny way?

SWAYING THROUGH LIFE

The body knows things the mind cannot grasp. This is a truth recognized across cultures and disciplines and throughout history. When we witness how movement, and particularly dance, reshapes people's lives, we're seeing evidence of an ancient wisdom that science is only beginning to explain.

Dancer Marisa Hamamoto's relationship with movement shifted drastically after she experienced a spinal stroke that temporarily paralyzed her from the neck down in 2006. Doctors told her she might never walk again, let alone dance. After she miraculously recovered most of her mobility, this life-changing incident opened her to a new understanding of movement itself.

"Dance is a universal language that belongs to everyone. Anyone can experience the joy and benefits of dance, because joy is a human right," Marisa explains. This insight led her to found

Infinite Flow Dance, a dance company bringing together dancers with and without disabilities to create art based on the premise that "everyone has a dancer inside of them."

When Infinite Flow holds community events like flash mobs, Marisa witnesses how movement breaks down social barriers. People from all walks of life connect through dance, forming friendships that extend far beyond the dance floor. "There's something about moving that energy around your body that just makes the mind work more creatively," she explains.

For Tania Kottoor, Indian classical dance became a vessel for emotions too overwhelming to process through thought alone. Trained in bharatanatyam, Tania says, "When I performed onstage, it was a way for me to let out all the feelings that I was holding in."

The structure of dance offered her a safe container: "A lot of the dance involves storytelling, so I'd display a person who was feeling sad or angry and let it out. It was easier to release because it was part of the choreography—depersonalized."

This power of embodied release appeared dramatically at her wedding, where family tensions had been building. "Just a few hours before, I felt like I was about to burst into tears, after our parents had given us a hard time," she recalls. "But when I stepped onto the dance floor, something shifted. I was so present, so playful with the audience, that I thought, 'Fuck it. I made it this far. I'm just going to be in the moment.' And all the pent-up anger melted away. I wasn't just performing. I was releasing."

When we exercise or even just move mindfully, our brains produce a protein scientists call "Miracle-Gro for the brain," because it helps neurons grow new connections and strengthens existing ones (Reynolds 2016).

This is why our best ideas often come during a walk, while showering, or while doing dishes—activities where we're moving but not consciously focused on problem-solving. The movement creates new neural pathways and connections—exactly what we need when we're creatively blocked or tangled up in thought loops.

When you're mentally gridlocked, remember these stories. Know that the solution might not be more thinking but getting out of your head entirely. Dance it out. Shake it off. Walk it through. Let your animal instincts lead you back to your natural state of flow, and watch as what seemed so complicated from inside your head suddenly becomes clear through the wisdom of your moving, sensing, knowing form.

SHAKING LOOSE IN THE WORKPLACE

If there's any place where we're conditioned to be floating heads—disconnected from our physical forms and trapped in our thoughts—it's the workplace. Our culture has convinced us that, in professional settings, our brains are all we're being paid for. Our flesh and bones? Just there to fill the chair.

So we disregard our bodies, and push on our brains, even more in work settings. I can't tell you how many times I've sat stubbornly at my desk, trying to force my brain to produce a genius idea, only to crank myself into a tighter and tighter spot. My physical self clenches, my breathing shallows, and I find myself in a different kind of blob state: not passive, but actively stuck, like spinning wheels digging deeper into mud. Often, I think, "I should probably go for a walk or take a little break," but then the stubbornness kicks in, and I say, "No, you can't take a break *until* you come up with the idea."

What nonsense! Of course, the minute I release this pressure on my brain and get moving, things loosen up, and ideas start to flow. The blocked state and the flowing state aren't just mental conditions—they're physical ones too. When we're in our heads, we're usually stagnant in our bodies as well, lacking momentum, wound tight.

I discovered the power of breaking this pattern leading creative teams at Refinery29. In meetings where we needed fresh thinking, I noticed how everyone (myself included) would arrive carrying the tension of their last conversation, deadline pressure, or inbox overwhelm—all that stress visibly living in hunched shoulders, furrowed brows, and tightly crossed arms.

So I started doing something that initially raised eyebrows: improv-style shake-outs at the beginning of meetings. I'd stand up and announce, "Before we start, we're going to shake off whatever we brought into this room!" Then I'd loudly count down—"Five, four, three, two, one!"—while we all shook our right arms, then left arms, right legs, left legs, five times each, then four, three, two, and finally one.

It. Felt. Silly. That was precisely the point. The first time I did this, people looked at me like I'd lost my mind. But as the fearless leader, I went first—flailing my limbs with abandon, laughing at myself. Soon enough, everyone joined in. By the end, the energy in the room had completely reconfigured. No one was "cool" anymore. We were just humans, together, a little embarrassed, a little energized, and lot more present.

These physical shake-outs went beyond silliness. They were strategic tools to get us out of our heads. They shook loose the residue of the last meeting, released stress that was blocking original thinking, and brought us into the present moment together. And from that place of embodied presence, our connections and ideas flowed more naturally.

The science backs me up here. Movement doesn't just give our thinking brains a break; it actually engages different neural networks, allowing new connections to form. When we're glued to our chairs, mentally spinning our wheels, we're cutting ourselves off from our full brainpower.

I'd end meetings with high-five circles. We'd stand up and gather 'round, and each person would high-five the person to their left and right simultaneously, in rapid succession. During the pandemic, we even did this on Zoom, extending virtual high-fives to our screens. It sounds cheesy, but it worked—that physical gesture, even when simulated, created a moment of connection and celebration that carried into our next tasks.

I've since used these techniques in my consulting work and play workshops, and the results are consistently powerful. Something as simple as intentional movement breaks the spell of disconnection that professional settings cast on us.

So, what can you do in professional settings where movement isn't the norm?

Start small. Bring colored pens to your next meeting and doodle while listening. Research shows this actually improves retention rather than being a distraction (Andrade 2009). Take your one-on-one meetings for a walk instead of sitting across a table. Suggest a five-minute stretch break during long sessions. Or be bold and introduce a quick shake-out ritual to your team.

Remember, in workplaces where we're expected to be buttoned up in our Serious Suits, even small movements can be revolutionary. We're not just thinking machines. We're living, breathing, moving beings with wisdom that extends far beyond our analytical minds. Your body is waiting to help you, if only you'll let it.

DANCING THROUGH SADNESS IN MY HAPPY PLACE

Movement isn't just for creative blocks or work meetings—it can be a lifeline during our most challenging emotional moments.

One spectacularly sunny August day, I was visiting my parents at home in Maine. My mom and I were getting ready to take my daughter to the beach, stuffing towels and snacks into a tote bag, when a truck pulled into the driveway. I was surprised to see my dad get out of the passenger side. It was unlike him to come back from work early, and it was strange that he wasn't in his own car.

Without going into the details, our family was abruptly facing a health scare. The calm summer day evolved into anxious phone calls, a rushed hospital visit, and a night of uncertainty. Tests were run, but answers remained elusive. My mind raced with worst-case scenarios, and the weight of worry settled heavy on my shoulders.

The next day, we had plans to take my daughter to my favorite childhood amusement park, Funtown Splashtown USA, which seemed ridiculous given the circumstances, but my parents insisted we not disappoint her just to wallow in anxiety, so my mom, my partner, and I went to Funtown.

I did my best to try to have fun, to ride rides and run around with my little one—to create a fun memory for her in this storied place of my childhood—but under the surface, I was a worry stew. The crashing of the bumper cars, dinging bells of the kiddie boats, and shrieks of kids on the roller coaster were nerve jangling. My nervous system was on the brink of bubbling over, and it was taking all I had to hold the lid on.

As I stood there trying to keep my shit together, a song came on the amusement park speaker system, and UB40 sang smoothly about red, red wine. The next thing I knew, my partner, Philippe, was reaching for my hand to dance. His hand hovered in the air, and I hesitated to grasp on to it. My heart weighed a thousand pounds and I wasn't particularly in a dancing mood, but the courage of his act pulled at my heartstrings. Of the two of us, I am one thousand times more likely to dance in public than he is, so it was bold and loving that he was willing to be silly in public for my benefit.

I accepted and waltzed around Funtown with him, hand in hand, my head on his shoulder, feeling ridiculous but also deeply held. As we danced, a wave of gratitude washed over me. His gesture was a lifeline thrown to me in a sea of worry and a reminder that sometimes the most profound moments of connection happen wordlessly through the physical invitation to play.

There is huge generosity in gently inviting someone to play when they're down. It's not about ignoring the pain or pretending everything is okay. Rather, it's about creating a moment of respite, a pocket of joy amid the sorrow. It's a way of saying, "I see your pain, and I'm here with you in it."

There are countless ways we can extend this invitation to others. If someone is grieving, you might offer to take a walk with them in nature, maybe even suggesting a game of "I spy" to gently engage their senses. For a friend going through a breakup, you could suggest a karaoke night where you can belt out heartbreak anthems together. For a family member dealing with illness, you could bring over a jigsaw puzzle and work on it together while chatting. Or for a child anxious about starting at a new school, maybe you have a pillow fort building session where you can talk about their fears in a safe, playful space.

These irreverent, physical gestures don't solve the underlying problems, but they offer a moment of connection, a breath of fresh air in stifling circumstances. They remind us that joy and sorrow can coexist and that we can move through them together.

As Philippe and I twirled around Funtown, my anxiety didn't disappear, but it loosened its grip. In that dance, I remembered that no matter what challenges lay ahead, I wasn't facing them alone. And sometimes, that knowledge—along with a little bit of play—is enough to help us take the next step forward.

MOVING THROUGH UNCERTAINTY

At the end of 2020, the world was in a suspended state, and so was I. My step count told the story: I went from walking an average of eleven thousand steps a day (I'm a New Yorker!) to a measly two thousand. I was a new mom with a toddler at home, facing a huge career change as the end of my time at Refinery29 drew near.

My work had been such a huge part of my identity for fifteen years—people often introduced me as "Piera from Refinery29" like it was my full legal name. Motherhood was already shifting how I saw myself, and now I wondered: Who would I be without this professional title I'd held for so long?

The uncertainty of big transitions can be destabilizing. They force you to ask those annoyingly profound questions, like "Who am I?" "What do I have to offer?" "Where to next?" "What do I want?" These existential pop quizzes beg you to really dive deep inside yourself to find answers but, frustratingly, often highlight your lack of clarity before they shed light on anything useful. As I asked these questions, I was met with a big, fat "I don't know" that echoed through my anxious mind.

In a normal world, I might have thrown a raucous goodbye party and jetted off on some soul-searching adventure. But that was not in the cards. I felt anxious and boxed in by pandemic life, unsure how I was going to process the change, let alone get clarity on what was next for my career. I needed a bridge to take me into the unknown future but I was trapped in my head, trying to think my way out of a problem that thinking couldn't solve.

My friend Debbie Attias had created a cathartic, playful dance form called Dancorcism and she advertised a teacher training workshop. With zero intention of becoming a dance instructor, I decided to sign up anyway. For eight weeks, I joined virtual trainings with a small group of strangers where I learned about dance, somatic release, and creating environments where people can freely express themselves through movement. Most important, each week, we *danced* together, trying out different moves, breathing techniques, and choreography homework that stretched my creativity in entirely new ways. For the first time in months, I was really alive, vibrating with energy.

One of the most beautiful things was getting to know these people through their movements, watching their unique personalities and styles come to life in how they danced. None of us saw ourselves as professional dancers, but we each truly had our own way of moving. There was Sebas, who would dramatically pantomime slipping on sexy gloves. Renata had us headbanging to punk rock like angry teenagers. Kirsten taught us gentler movements, like "scrubbing our energy" with imaginary soapy sponges. It was like I knew these people at a cellular level despite never having met most of them in person. I knew them because we had danced together.

Movement disrupts the endless loops of rumination that trap us in our heads. It shifts our attention away from worrying to witnessing, from our thoughts to our sensations. That's exactly what was happening: My rumination about who I was now was being interrupted by the simple joy of noticing my body move through space. I was playing in the truest sense and creating something just for the joy of it, fully immersed in the moment, with that distinctive lightness that comes when we're truly at play.

To get certified, I had to teach two classes (gulp). I texted close friends and family to join and prepared my playlist and choreography for my debut performance as a dance instructor. My mom, my best high school buddy, a few favorite coworkers, and my friends' family joined. I put a disco ball in my family room, propped my computer on my toddler's desk, and fired up the Zoom dance room.

What happened next was unexpected. I was suddenly buzzing with energy and love, the truest version of myself. When I taught dance, I had no questions about who I was—it was absolutely clear to me in a way that all my cerebral agonizing had never revealed. So I decided to continue. I put it out on Instagram: "Would anyone want to join my Dancorcism class? DM me if so!" To my shock, two hundred and fifty people DMed me that day. Two hundred and fifty people wanted to dance with me! In a pandemic! Through screens!

For nine months, I taught three classes a week to thousands of people around the world as a gift of joy. We danced on Christmas when a new COVID variant meant I couldn't go home to see my parents. We danced in the New Year across global time zones. We did Friday nights at "Club Zoom."

The messages I received from participants still make me emotional. One comment in particular struck me: "I've been dealing with depression lately, finding it really hard to move or create anything, and your class today is the most fun I've had in weeks, also the most connected, free, and happy I've felt in a while." I knew exactly what they meant. After months of stagnant isolation and distance, moving together reconnected us to our inner selves and each other. As one sweating and smiling attendee pointed out, this class was "a reset button for our lives during these tough times."

Through it all, I found myself—beyond the identity of my career or my role as a mom. I discovered my essence, my spirit self. (As cheesy as that sounds!) This essential version of me is always there, no matter what else happens in my life or the world.

By getting out of my head and into my body, I joyfully twirled, bounced, and flowed through a period of deep anxiety and global and personal uncertainty. When I couldn't think my way to answers, my body showed me the way. The answers weren't in my head—they were in my hips, my arms, my jumping feet, my twirling hands.

Movement doesn't just shift energy. It can shift perspective, relationships, identity, and possibility. When we're contained and constrained by circumstances or our own swirling thoughts, the simple act of physical release can create unexpected openings. Sometimes the path forward isn't something you figure out—it's something you dance your way into.

Your "Move Out of Your Head" Toolkit
Develop Your Mover and Shaker Powers

The Flash Recap: When we're stuck in our heads, movement reconnects us to our bodies, unlocking creativity, deepening connection, and inviting joy. Physical play shifts our energy, dissolves mental blocks, and allows us to connect with ourselves and others on a level beyond words. Even the smallest movements can create profound shifts, allowing our playful spirits to emerge in a world that keeps us sitting still.

Wiggle Room: When transitioning between tasks today, take ten seconds to roll your shoulders, circle your wrists, or stretch your neck. These micromovements create natural breaks in your thought patterns and bring you back to your body.

Play Practice
The Shake Break

One-song movement reset to shift your energy

When you're spinning your wheels or in a slump, this quick movement practice helps you switch up your state. By dedicating just a few minutes to uninhibited movement, you create a physical and mental reset for yourself (and those around you).

How to Practice

1. Notice when you're feeling stuck or low-energy.
2. Pick a song that will shift your energy.
3. Move freely for the entire song without self-judgment.
4. Start small (shoulder rolls, head nods) and allow the movement to grow organically.
5. Notice the shift in your energy when the song ends.

Shake Break Variations

- **Social:** Use the Shake Break as a group energizer or family reset button
- **Micro Moves:** If mobility is limited, tap rhythms, doodle to the beat, or move just upper body
- **Story Dance:** Get literal and pantomime the lyrics as the song plays
- **Release Party:** Imagine throwing off stress or shaking off unwanted feelings with each move
- **Follow the Leader:** Let one body part lead your moves

Even the smallest movements create change, so adapt the practice to what you can do in the moment. The goal isn't to look good but to physically disrupt patterns and reconnect with your physical self. You don't need to be a dancer or athlete, you just need to be ready to shake things up, literally and figuratively, for the length of one song.

Build a playlist with songs for different moods, and use Shake Breaks as transition rituals throughout your day—between tasks, switching from work to home, or whenever you need a reset.

What wild delights
might you discover

If your attention you could recover?

A rainbow in a hydrant's mist

A little thing you might
have missed

Look up, look down, zoom in to see

The patterned wings of bumblebee

Renew your wows and see each day

Through baby's eyes
wowooogahyay*

*read this in baby's babbling voice

CHAPTER 7

Renew Your Wows

Observe curiously and watch the world come alive

The universe is full of magical things, patiently waiting for our wits to grow sharper.

Eden Phillpotts

In any given moment, in any place, there are countless fascinating things to observe, if only we get curious enough to look for them. The Wonder Wanderers among us are well practiced in this art of noticing.

Wherever you are now, take a few seconds to look around and see if you can find one thing that you haven't noticed before. For real, do it!

It could be as subtle as a curiously shaped shadow, the quality of light streaming through the window, or as obvious as a stranger's eye-catching outfit. Now take a few breaths, relax, and see what you observe about yourself. How does your body feel? Are you warm or cold? What mood are you in?

By focusing your awareness, you took a baby step toward becoming more observant.

This practice of noticing allows you to appreciate your surroundings and is also the foundation of original thinking and innovation. When we train ourselves to notice what others miss, we're building our creative muscles and filling up an inspiration reservoir we can draw from later.

Such a simple thing, right? But in our fast-paced, technology-driven world, it takes extra effort to wrestle it back into our own hands. But the payoff is worth it. By grabbing our viewfinder and pointing it at awe and amazement, we amplify those forces in our lives.

So, take my hand, we're going to the beach to get our amazement back.

A BEACHCOMBER'S EYE

As a little girl growing up on the coast of Maine, one of my most beloved things to do was go down to the rocky beach by my house and walk, looking for tiny delights. My ears filled with the sound of the waves, the whoosh and clatter of the ocean slurping up rocks and spitting them back out onto the beach in a soothing rhythm. I'd tread carefully between the tide pools, my eyes trained on the pebbled ground, my small body stooped. The salty air whipped around me as I slowly made my way forward, scanning the ground, searching for surprises.

I was on high alert for a translucent glow, pops of color, or incongruous patterns to tip me off to a treasure's presence. Then, something would catch my eye. I'd crouch down, gently brushing aside the smaller stones to reveal my discovery. I'd pick it up, admiring this precious object in my palm, and add it to the growing collection in my pocket.

Onward I'd go, my movements measured and intentional. The element of chance, of imminent surprise, propelled me forward in this pursuit—the delight of knowing that any day could be the day that I found a rare piece of blue sea glass or a perfect, round sand dollar.

When I beachcomb, I am connected to what is immediately in front of me. The tumble of tiny rocks and shells. The vast ocean that brought these little treasures to my toes. I'm part of something larger, yet grounded in the here and now, my senses heightened as I search.

Now I realize this was my child meditation—finding fascination in the present moment.

The handy thing about a beachcomber's eye is that you can use it anywhere: at your desk, on the subway, or in your backyard. It's the practice of being on the lookout for beauty and deeming things "treasure" that others might see as ordinary.

WONDER WANDERS

My beachcomber's eye has taken new form in adulthood. I often take myself (and groups of people) out on what I call Wonder Wanders. I tell myself I'm going on a treasure hunt and that I'm tuning my awareness (like a radio dial) to the frequency of fascination and delight. I tap into my senses and obey that tried-and-true guidance that we know but rarely adhere to: Stop to smell the flowers, stop to touch grass. It's a walk where I try to just notice, be amused, and get into my senses.

I started doing Wonder Wanders during a particularly difficult period of depression. Living with major depressive disorder and seasonal affective disorder means there are times when my internal light dims, my inner voice becomes punishing, and my natural enthusiasm for life ebbs away. In those moments, even getting out of the house can seem overwhelming. But I've learned that these simple walks can be a gentle way to reengage with the world when I'm in a sunken place. They don't require forced cheerfulness, they're just about noticing: a leaf, a shadow, a snippet of music floating from an open window. Sometimes that's enough to create a tiny crack in the heaviness, to remind me that the world is still there, still interesting, still worth connecting with.

These intentional observation strolls get us moving and give our brains a different kind of exercise. Rachel and Stephen Kaplan, professors of psychology, teach that nature provides the perfect balance of "soft fascination"—sights, sounds, and sensations that we notice gently without overwhelming us. This effortless engagement allows your mind to wander and recover from the exhausting attention that screens and technology demand. Nature doesn't have to be somewhere totally wild and isolated either, even looking up at the sky or down at a patch of grass can do the trick.

A Wonder Wander might be its own meandering activity or layered onto an errand or task. Either way, the mission is simple: to find awe in plain sight and discover things you usually miss when you're on autopilot. I look up, at the sky, the tops of the buildings, the birds on the electric lines. I also look down, at the chalk hopscotch course drawn on the sidewalk by neighbors or the dandelion that's managed to grow out of a hairline crack in the cement. Sometimes I'll zoom in close enough to see that the grass isn't a smooth blade, as it first seemed, but is traversed by fine lines and membranes. I approach my surroundings as if I'm seeing them for the first time and tune in to my senses: the sights, sounds, smells, and sensations. Sometimes I'll close my eyes for a minute and take in the layers of sound: the birds chirping, a snippet of conversation in the wind, the lapping of the river.

Our brains automatically filter information to help us function. At any given moment, we are consciously aware of less than 0.1 percent of sensory information (Agarwal 2020). That's why, when we pause to notice, we open a portal to the other 99.9 percent of wonder in the world. This can feel like a magic trick or a shock to the system. We can be so absorbed in our noisy minds and worlds that we are completely unaware of the texture of a moment. Even as someone who works to cultivate my consciousness, I'm often amazed by how much I fail to notice.

Outside of the mental health benefits I experience, these walks fill my unexpected creative well. I'll find words or phrases to inspire a bit of copywriting, image references for a campaign I'm creative directing, or notice human behavior that might wind up in an essay I'm writing. Observation is the foundation of so many new inventions, works of art, and scientific pursuits, after all. Noticing is an act of surrender, a decentering of self, an acceptance of the element of surprise. Who knows what we'll discover when we are open to inspiration arriving at any moment?

Before you leave the house, remember:

Keys

Wallet

Wonder

EVERY DAY IS A FIRST

One of my artistic role models, Suleika Jaouad, is a sharp and honest observer of herself and the world. She's the author of the *New York Times* bestselling memoir *Between Two Kingdoms*, and a self-described alchemist, transforming challenges into creative beauty.

When I spoke with Suleika, she told me that when she was twenty-two years old, just as she was starting her adult life, she was diagnosed with leukemia. Amid grueling treatments and terrifying uncertainty, Suleika felt deeply stuck. She was angry that she was in a hospital while her friends were starting their careers, falling in love, and dancing all night long. But from that challenging space, she reconnected with her powers of observation in a way that became her lifeline.

To create a sense of daily purpose, she took on a hundred-day project centered on noticing. She began to write about the small details of hospital life—the rhythms of the nurses' shifts, the play of light on the walls, the emotions flickering across her visitors' faces. She had dreamed of being a war correspondent, and as she wrote her daily dispatches in her journal, she imagined she was, only her conflict zone was the cancer ward.

Through her keen eye and original spirit, Suleika started a blog that became a *New York Times* column, "Life, Interrupted"; an Emmy award–winning video series; and later, her memoir. More important, they kept her connected to the flow of life even amid the most suspended of circumstances.

Suleika went into remission when she was twenty-six, but then in her early thirties, her leukemia returned. Her doctor sat her down and told her that, though she was doing well, she could expect to be in some kind of treatment or other indefinitely. To not have an ending in sight to her suffering was an enormous blow.

Her doctor kept telling her over and over again that she had to live every day like it was her last. It's common advice and she knew he was well-meaning, but the pressure was overwhelming. Suleika panicked every time he said it, asking herself, "How do I wring that much life and meaning out of every day, every interaction?" It was a spiritually exhausting way to live and also completely unsustainable.

So instead, she adopted this gentler mindset: trying to live every day as if it's her first—"to try to wake up and meet the day with the sense of curiosity and wonder and playfulness that a newborn baby might." She thinks about what is wondrous to a little kid. "It's not some epic bucket list item. It can be a bug scuttling through the grass, and that's fascinating and delightful and funny. That shift in mindset has been so helpful."

By bringing those beginner's eyes to each sunup and each sundown, Suleika has managed to be in deeper engagement with her life—finding fascination and glimmers of delight in small moments—and bringing together thousands of others with this open-hearted, curious way of living. She demonstrates how in suspended moments we can find solace in the simple act of paying attention.

THE LENS YOU CHOOSE

Our attention is the most valuable currency we possess. Where we spend it creates our experience of being alive.

One spring morning, I woke up feeling weight on my chest, dreading the day ahead. I was scheduled for an ob-gyn visit after years of infertility treatments and surgeries, carrying past pain and anxiety with me. Afterward, I'd be clearing out my office belongings—the end of a long career chapter.

I texted my friend Katia, telling her about my bummer Friday plans, and said: "I need a little extra love today." Instead of offering the expected sympathy, she replied cheerfully, "What would today look like through the lens of love?"

My first reaction was annoyance. What toxic positivity bs is this?! I wanted commiseration, not a challenge. But my friend Katia is wise and the question burrowed in (as good questions do!), and reluctantly, I decided to try it.

Heading to the doctor, I began observing with this new lens. I saw two silvery blue pigeons snuggled together on an electrical wire overhead, cooing. Next, I spotted a wall of dripping, rainbow colored graffiti hearts. Then my heart warmed to see an elderly couple making their way down the street hand in hand. Someone on the phone passed me saying, "I love you soooo much!" in a singsong voice. "Okay, I see you, love," I thought.

At the doctor's office, I centered on being my kindest self. I gave a big smile as I stepped up to the reception desk. "How's your day going?" I asked as they checked me in. The receptionist flashed a grin, "Great. What about you, sweetie?" It felt like a hug. In the exam room, I greeted the doctor like an old friend, asking about her kids. I thought about all the care she'd given me and how much I had been through, feeling tenderness and gratitude for my resilient spirit.

At my former workplace, where I'd expected melancholy packing in an empty office thanks to the lingering pandemic, I discovered Felicia, our beloved office manager, was there. We stood in the doorway to my office and talked for a long time. As we reminisced about funny office moments, I was overcome with unexpected laughter. Cleaning out my desk, I found a trove of handwritten thank-you notes, a gigantic birthday card my team had made me, and joyful photographs with coworkers that sparked joyful memories.

This supposedly dreaded day was reshaped through the simple act of redirecting my attention. The challenges remained the same—medical issues persisted as did the grief for the end of an era—but I had opened myself to being surprised by moments of connection and joy I might have otherwise missed.

The lens through which we observe creates the world we experience. This doesn't mean ignoring difficult emotions or forcing positivity. It means recognizing that even on our hardest days, we can redistribute a fraction of our attention to notice what might surprise us. The act of looking itself—observing with openness rather than assumption—creates space for wonder to enter, even in unlikely places.

When you think about it, attention is the ultimate form of love. From childhood onward, nothing signals being loved so much as receiving undivided attention. Where you place your attention is where you give your love.

NOW, ARE YOU READY TO RENEW YOUR WOWS?

In her poem "When Death Comes," Mary Oliver imagines a life spent "married to amazement." What would it mean to live that way—to take the whole messy, beautiful world into your arms with full attention, wild appreciation, and committed wonder?

Paying attention is an act of generosity and love, a way of saying "I see you" to the world, to the people around you, and to yourself. In every moment, there is something worth noticing, something worth appreciating, something worth being amazed by.

So, are you ready to RENEW YOUR WOWS?

Renew Your Wows

I vow to look up from my phone and catch the magic show happening around me.

I vow to label things that delight me as "treasure."

I vow to be curious and open to surprise.

I vow to remember that each day is a first.

I vow to be wowed.

Your "Renew Your Wows" Toolkit
Develop Your Wonder Wanderer Powers

The Flash Recap: Wonder Wanderers know that magic isn't hidden in faraway places; it's right here, waiting to be noticed. By approaching each day with fresh eyes, we uplift ordinary moments to extraordinary discoveries. The practice of paying attention enriches our lives and sparks creativity.

Wiggle Room: As you brush your teeth tonight, focus on one sensory element you normally ignore—the sound of the water, the sensation of the brush bristles, or the taste of the toothpaste. Fascination lives in these everyday sensations we've learned to filter out.

Play Practice
Wonder Wanders

Scavenger hunts for awe and delight

Transform any walk or commute into a treasure hunt by searching for the glimpses of delight hiding in plain sight. Imagine you're tuning your frequency to the "wow" channel, like a baby seeing the world for the first time. Rather than focusing on getting somewhere, notice where you are along the way.

How to Practice

1. Designate a walk or commute as a Wonder Wander.
2. Set an intention to notice with fresh eyes and engage all senses.
3. Choose a mission from the list or follow your curiosity.
4. Slow your pace to allow for discovery.
5. Photograph, share, or journal one surprising find.

Missions

- Color Hunt: Collect all the pinks (or yellows, greens, blues) you can spot.
- Zoom Focus: Take in the smallest details you can spot and the widest views.
- Sensory Spotlight: Let smell, sound, or touch lead your exploration.
- Seasonal Savor: Take in the unique hallmarks of the season.
- Signs and Symbols: Hunt for patterns, messages, and signs.

Modifications

Window-gazing works well if walking is challenging or outdoor access is limited. A single view offers endless shifts in light, weather, and passing activity. Indoor spaces work too—light patterns moving across floors, the angles of household objects, or the miniature worlds happening in your houseplants.

If you process the world differently, lean into your strengths. Visual processing challenging? Sound mapping or texture exploration through touch can become your primary tools for noticing.

These practices aren't about achieving a specific experience. They're about working with what you have, where you are, using whatever abilities feel accessible to you.

CHAPTER 8

Try It and See

Experiment Your Way Through the Unknown

Consider everything an experiment. Nothing is a mistake. There's no win and no fail, there's only make.

Corita Kent

In life's grand lab, we mix and brew

Is this thing on? Testing, one, two

No win or loss, just lessons learned

Each experience a page
we've turned

With curiosity as our guide

We explore and stumble,
know we tried

For in each risk and bold endeavor

We've grown and changed,
our stories better

Picture walking into a kindergarten classroom, arms laden with tubes of vibrant paint and an assortment of brushes. You ask, "Who wants to paint?" The response is immediate and enthusiastic. They dive in, squeezing out colors, mixing with abandon, exploring, and creating joyful messes on their papers.

This scene is a window into the experimental mindset of the Curious Quester, whose gift is turning questions and uncertainties into experiments. This childlike spirit that asks "What if?" allows us to take on new challenges and expand.

But as we get older, something shifts. That fearless, curious child morphs into an adult frozen by the fear of making mistakes. We become so terrified of messing up that we often don't even try. We tell ourselves, "I don't want to look foolish," or "There are experts who can do it better than me, so why bother?" The thought "What if I fail?!" turns us into a puddle of worry melted on the floor.

This fear of uncertainty stalls us. We'd rather stay in control and do nothing than risk stepping into the unknown, even if that means missing opportunities for learning and joy.

As the Curious Questers among us know, life doesn't stop being an experiment just because we've grown up. When we embrace our inner curiosity and turn our pursuits into experiments, we activate our discovery drive and make new connections. These powers help us move past perfectionism and fear, turning uncertainty from a threat into a playground.

IT'S NOT EASY LEARNING TO CRAWL

I watch my baby, her chubby face scrunched in effort. She's on her belly, arms and legs splayed, like a starfish on the living room rug. For weeks, she's been trying to crawl, each attempt a miniature experiment in physics and human anatomy.

Kick with the legs. A slight scoot forward. Push with the arms. Chest goes up. Face-plant into the carpet. Pause. Try again.

As I look at her, I'm struck by how much effort this takes.

We think of milestones like crawling as inevitable waypoints on the road of development, but it's not always cute. There's massive frustration. There are tears. There are moments when her expression clearly says, "Mom, this floor isn't working. Can you fix it?" Yet she keeps going: testing, failing, adjusting, trying again.

As adults, we often forget this lesson. Our fixed thinking convinces us that if we can't control the outcome or guarantee success, we shouldn't try at all. We become rigid where we once were fluid. We try something once, and when it doesn't work, we throw in the towel. "I'm just not cut out for this," we say, as if one failed attempt proves our inadequacy. But imagine if a baby gave up after their first crawling attempt.

When someone enters their "stretch zone"—that sweet spot between comfort and panic—that's where true expansion happens. It's a space of productive discomfort where we're challenged but not overwhelmed. For the baby, comfort is lying still, while being placed standing before she's ready might cause panic. Crawling sits right in that perfect middle ground.

As she rocks back and forth, pushing with arms and legs, she's stretching beyond what's comfortable. This process isn't always smooth. There are tears, stuck points, and frustrations, but in these moments of stretch, new neural pathways form, muscles strengthen, and confidence builds.

The same principle applies to us. When we deliberately place ourselves in our stretch zone—whether learning a new skill, having a difficult conversation, or tackling a challenging project—we're emulating that determined baby. We're saying yes to growth, even when it's uncomfortable.

If you saw yourself as a baby learning to crawl, would you look at your struggle and yell, "What a LOSER!"? No, that would be totally fucked up! But—tell the truth—does your internal monologue turn harsh when you fail at something new? If so, it's time to change the narrative. Like a baby, you deserve the grace to be a beginner, a stretch-zoner, an experimenter.

This is where curiosity becomes our greatest ally against harsh self-judgment. When we approach something with genuine curiosity ("I wonder what would happen if I tried this?"), we naturally suspend judgment. The curious mind doesn't preclassify experiences as successes or failures; it simply collects observations with openness and interest. Like a scientist watching an experiment unfold, we become observers of our own experience rather than critics of our performance.

If ever you bristle at the discomfort, tell yourself: "I'm not flailing; I'm just stretching!"

BE THE EXPERIMENTER

Little Camilla Pang, wide-eyed and curious, was kicking piles of autumn leaves over and over again. To the casual observer, it might have looked like simple play. But for Camilla Pang, this wasn't just fun—it was science in action.

"I would do it repetitively in order to find the laws about how things react and how they can be predicted," Camilla told me, her expressive eyebrows dancing as she spoke. Each kick was a data point, each explosion of brown and orange a result to be analyzed. Through this exploration, young Camilla was gradually building a map of how the world worked.

As a kid, Camilla was sure she'd landed on the wrong planet, "like a stranger within [her] own species." Social cues and communication with other people felt foreign, and she asked her mom if there was "an instruction manual for humans." There wasn't one, so Camilla turned to science and playful experimentation to create her own.

"You are the experimenter," she told herself. This simple yet powerful mantra became her guiding principle, changing everyday challenges into curiosity-fueling experiments. "When you experiment, there are no personal failures—only results." Some results might not be what you expected, but they're all valuable data.

As she grew older, her experiments evolved. She filled notebook upon notebook with scientific concepts and observations about people, with diagrams full of arrows and spirals, wavy lines, questions, and flows.

"Over time, it became bigger, and notebooks piled up," Camilla recalled.

The way Camilla turned life into a series of experiments wasn't just about understanding the world. It was about finding her place in it. At a young age, she had learned that the world wasn't designed for her unique way of thinking as a person on the autism spectrum with ADHD. Rather than trying to fit into a mold that didn't suit her, she turned to science and play.

Eventually, after much observation and experimentation—and after earning her PhD—she created the guidebook she had asked for as a child. Her memoir, *An Outsider's Guide to Humans: What Science Taught Me About What We Do and Who We Are*, was her way of making sense out of a confusing world. The ripple effect of her experimentation is that her findings—now in book form—are helping thousands of other people make sense of the world.

Camilla's approach is so powerful because it reframes uncertainty from something to fear into something to explore. Instead of being attached to specific outcomes, she focuses on the process of discovery itself.

The Experimental Method

Begin with curiosity: Ask questions that you don't have answers for... yet.
Form hypotheses: Come up with ideas about how things might work based on what you already know.
Design simple tests: Create small experiments to test your ideas.
Observe without judgment: Record what happens with an open mind, seeing unexpected outcomes as valuable data, not failures.
Iterate and refine: Build on what you've learned in each experiment, gradually improving your understanding.
Turn uncertainty into wonder: Approach confusing situations as fascinating research opportunities rather than threats.
Break free from perfectionism: Find freedom in the experimental process rather than fixating on perfect outcomes.

QUESTING, QUESTING, ONE TWO THREE

Life's transitions and in-between moments can feel destabilizing. We're tempted to make bold declarations of certainty, to lock ourselves into a clear path forward, just to escape the discomfort of not knowing. But curiosity rewards us much more than certainty ever could.

In the bustling, gray city of London, Sam Furness felt burned out, uninspired—like he had lost his magic. Stuck in his job managing bands, he yearned for his own independent creative expression. Instead of quitting his job or reinventing his life, he decided to embark on a mission to pursue one new or challenging thing each month in his spare time. He called these his "creative quests": mini adventures that prioritized learning and exploration over perfection or mastery.

January was spent learning origami, folding paper cranes that then flew through the sky of his bedroom ceiling. In February, he studied flight patterns of birds and spent lunch breaks folding paper airplanes with colleagues. In March, he drew everything in the world around him.

By the end of the year, though much of his life looked the same—same city, same job—it was as if a whole new realm of possibility had opened, like he'd been on a trip around the world and returned home with a fresh perspective on his life. Though it started as a year-long project, it became a practice that continued over a decade, radically reshaping his life and connecting him to many others who have joined him in questing.

New mother Linda Armstrong faced overwhelming uncertainty navigating postpartum depression and the learning curve of early motherhood. Instead of expecting herself to have it all figured out, she reframed each outing with her baby as "practice." As she struggled to connect the car seat to the stroller or nurse in a public space, she'd say out loud to herself, "Oh, this is just practice." This experimental mindset gave her permission to learn through experience and eventually find her confidence as a mom, recognizing how much she'd learned in her "practice" phase.

When entrepreneur Mayssa Chehata got out of the corporate world, she pinned everything on her fledgling candy business, Behave, being her golden ticket to financial freedom. But she got so attached to her timelines and goals that every production delay, bad review, or "no" from a store would send her off the rails emotionally.

She found herself in a dark place, crying after investor calls and feeling disconnected from her joyful product. Things drastically shifted when she started seeing her business as a laboratory, rather than a test of her worth. Instead of stubbornly defending her existing formula, she started trying new flavors and asking for honest feedback. She created a list of ten changes that had to happen in six months or she'd shut down. "I thought there was no way we'd accomplish them all," Mayssa said. "But when we shifted into playfulness and creative problem-solving instead of rigid strategy, the answers revealed themselves." They checked every item off the list, and more importantly, she found the sweetness in her business again.

Neuroscientist Anne-Laure Le Cunff's research validates this approach. Her book *Tiny Experiments* explains how our brains physically change when we adopt an experimental mindset. Each time we try something new, we create new neural pathways, reshaping our brains (Le Cunff 2025).

Le Cunff suggests reframing what she calls "in-between moments"—those uncertain transitions in life—as growth moments. Instead of seeing them as uncomfortable periods to rush through, we can view them as laboratories for experimentation.

When we approach life this way, the brain's threat response (centered in the amygdala) calms down. Meanwhile, the prefrontal cortex—responsible for problem-solving and creativity—becomes more active. In other words, experimentation isn't only a smoother approach, it makes our brains work better.

All of these Curious Questers were willing to prioritize discovery over certainty, learning over being right. When we frame our lives as experiments rather than tests, we free ourselves from the tyranny of perfectionism.

LOW-STAKES LIFE SIMULATIONS

Sometimes life's stakes feel too high to experiment freely. That's when we need practice grounds that are consequence-free.

Gamers have figured this out. People use the video game *The Sims* as a life simulator to test out major decisions, building digital storefronts of dream businesses before building physical shops, practicing flirting, or caring for virtual animals to test the waters of pet ownership before adopting real-life kitties. Others explore gender identity through role-playing games like Dungeons & Dragons, using the fictional environment to test social interactions and self-expression. Language learners practice new tongues in Animal Crossing.

These virtual worlds provide consequence-free zones to experiment with everything from career choices to social skills. What can make digital sandboxes so valuable is how they reframe failure. The "Game Over" screen isn't really the end—it's a chance to collect data, refine your strategy, and try again.

We can't magically respawn in real life when things go wrong. But we can adopt this gamer mindset, seeing each attempt as a chance to level up our skills and each setback as an opportunity to refine our approach.

MULTI-VERSE LIFE

A few years out of college, I sat across from an interviewer who asked about my five-year plan. I answered honestly and enthusiastically: "I don't have one, actually. I'm excited about exploring and growing my creative skills. I'm always inspired by people who have tried lots of different things and have great stories to tell!"

The interviewer looked displeased. I could see immediately

that this was NOT the right answer. Needless to say, I didn't get the job.

For years, I felt self-conscious about my non-linear approach. We could chalk it up to my ADHD brain, which naturally jumps between interests, or to my genuine belief that the most interesting lives are the multi-chaptered ones—full of plot twists and turns rather than a straight-line narrative.

While others had strategic plans, I experimented through life's in-between moments, trying new things to see what would stick. The scenes might be strange: crouching at fashion models' feet, tying their shoes for them, jumping up and down in Washington Square Park rallying people to dance, rubberizing boots in a basement while wearing a gas mask, dressed like a cigarette girl serving candy creations at a roller rink, painting rainbow stripes on a hundred-legged dog sculpture. (Like something out of a surreal dream sequence!)

My detours have had surprising applications. The thirteen years spent as a babysitter and nanny kept my child-like spirit alive and made me more creative. My time as a styling assistant taught me about trendspotting and dealing with clients. A stint as a party promoter was a lesson in inspiring people to show up. Most of these pursuits didn't become careers, side hustles, or even hobbies, but each gave me new experiences, inputs, and views.

When doubt crept in and I asked myself, "Where is this all going?" I'd return to my experimental mindset and comfort myself with the knowledge that I was learning by doing and that any seemingly random (or embarrassing) detour would at the very least make for a great future story.

This exploratory openness has created the kind of life I detailed in that job interview years ago. It might look confusing to other people expecting linear progression, but it felt exciting, enriching, and fantastically storied to me. Turns out the best plan can be no plan at all: just curiosity, courage, and a willingness to try it and see.

* * *

When we approach life as Curious Questers, saying "Let me try it and see," we free ourselves from the need to be sure and can find the joy of the process. Every experiment, whether it leads where we expected or not, becomes a worthy adventure.

The beauty of this mindset is that it's adaptable—you can experiment with a side project, a fifteen-minute daily practice, or a new approach within your existing job. The size of the experiment matters less than the curiosity and openness you bring to it.

You've made it this far in the book—you've unzipped your Serious Suit, renewed your wows, looked for pink flamingos, and moved out of your head. You've reclaimed so many dimensions of your playful spirit. I hope these stories and ideas have awakened curiosity sparks in you that are now eager to catch fire.

So, what will you try and see? What experiment is calling to you? What question is tugging at your sleeve, asking to be explored? Remember, you don't need to know the destination to head off on the journey. All you need is the courage to say "I wonder what would happen if . . ."

Your "Try It and See" Toolkit
Develop Your Curious Quester Powers

The Flash Recap: The Curious Quester thrives on experimentation, turning life's uncertainties into playful discoveries. By embracing an experimental mindset, you free yourself from perfectionism's grip and fear's freeze state, finding joy in the process rather than fixating on outcomes.

Wiggle Room: As you're getting dressed, consider one change you might make in how you present yourself and wonder how you might carry yourself differently if you did so. This small "what if" exercise gently stretches your experimentation muscles.

Play Practice
Try It Tuesdays

Weekly experiments in curiosity

Turn an ordinary Tuesday into a laboratory for living. This practice recognizes that growth happens at the edges of familiarity and that regular, manageable novelty is the antidote to autopilot living.

How to Practice

1. Designate Tuesday as your personal experiment day.
2. Keep a running list of things you'd be curious to try.
3. Each week, choose one small, doable experiment.
4. Set an intention for what you hope to learn or experience.
5. As you experiment, pay attention to what you discover.
6. Notice your responses, resistance, and insights.

Experiment Ideas

- **Identity Play:** Wear something that's "not you" but feels fun to try out, or introduce yourself with a new twist on your life story.

- **Routine Variation:** Take a different route, rearrange your morning sequence, or do things at a different pace than usual.
- **Sensory Shift:** Change the sensory ambiance of your environment with new lighting, scents, or object arrangement.
- **Taste Adventure:** Try a new recipe or a food or listen to a music genre you wouldn't usually.
- **Social Risk:** Initiate a conversation with someone you normally wouldn't or ask for help on something you'd usually handle alone.

Do your experiments solo or with other questers. Track patterns in what lights you up and what you resist. The value isn't in the experiments' magnitude but in the mindset of curiosity they develop. Each small risk builds your adaptability, reduces fear of the unknown, and reveals assumptions you didn't know you had.

CHAPTER 9

Don't Eat Yourself Alive!

Fuel Courage by Feeding It Self-Compassion

With compassion one becomes courageous.
                          The Tao Te Ching

To take on big feats,
you need to be fueled

Gas yourself up and try
not to be cruel

"Inner critic, shhhh!"
say it with zeal

Now, cheerleader side,
go ahead, take the wheel

On the road to courage,
self-compassion's your guide

So jump into kindness
and enjoy the ride!

We've almost reached the end of our journey together, and if there's one thing that's become crystal-clear throughout these pages, it's this: living playfully takes *guts*. That's because it requires a vulnerability, openness, and fluidity that is antithetical to how we're often told to be in this hard-edged world.

So, for this final chapter, I want to share what just might be the most essential skill of all. It's one we can use to strengthen all our other Powers of Play: self-compassion.

If we want to cultivate the courage to play, we have to become our own inner coach and cheerleader: rallying and consoling ourselves as we head into the field to play the game of life. The world may sneer and throw tomatoes at us from the stands, but we need to pick ourselves up, brush off the pulp, and say, "You did your best, sweet pea, keep playing."

Yet, too often, we do the opposite: We yell at ourselves, "You're cringe!" "You're terrible!" "You should give up!" That critical voice in our heads keeps a running tally of our perceived failures, whispering, "Not good enough," even when we're giving our all.

If that voice sounds all too familiar, you're not alone.

Many of us have been taught that harsh self-criticism is how we improve—and without constantly evaluating and judging ourselves, we'll stagnate. Entire industries profit from this message, selling us "stuff" to solve our inadequacies.

But this critic is keeping us from playing to our full potential. With some practice (I'll show you how), we can turn down the volume on that inner drill sergeant and amplify our inner cheerleader instead.

THE FAILURE LIST

In a box, buried beneath a pile of old notebooks and forgotten papers, I found a relic from a decade ago that punched me right in the gut. It was a list I'd made titled "Ways I'm Failing RN" and it read like a greatest-hits album of self-loathing.

Eleven items inventorying all the ways I wasn't living up to my sky-high expectations: Work projects. Fertility. Leadership. Friendships. Fitness. Family. And at the bottom: "Stressing myself out with my stress and inability to emotionally regulate."

I was eating myself alive with criticism, and this failure list was the evidence.

The irony? From the outside, I was at what appeared to be a career high point. I was leading a growing team, speaking at conferences, and building imaginative partnerships. But inside, I was burned out and brittle. No achievement scratched the itch of worthiness, no recognition filled the void. I was so busy judging my performance that I couldn't experience the joy in any of it.

My body began sending distress signals—insomnia, facial numbness, a perpetual knot in my stomach. One night, after lying on the floor of my apartment crying inconsolably about what a "failure" I was, it was clear that something had to give. My overworked, underplayed state had dried up all perspective and my spirit was in crumbs.

I'd like to tell you that I had an epiphany and started practicing self-compassion, and my problems melted away. But the truth was messier. I tried meditation and abandoned it after three days. I bought self-help books that gathered dust on my nightstand. I made schedules for "me time" that I immediately broke when work demands arose. These attempts just added "Can't fix myself" to the ongoing failure list in my head.

Gradually, though, small changes started to stick. I blocked fifteen minutes each morning to make coffee instead of getting it on the go. While it brewed, I'd scribble encouraging notes to myself on colorful index cards. Simple observations at first: "Hey, you're feeling overwhelmed." "You didn't get enough sleep last night, you might want to take it easier today." That grew into more of a dialogue: "You're giving so much creativity to work, what if you gave yourself permission to take a class and refill your cup?"

At first it felt a little cheesy writing to myself, but it also gave me a way of stopping to notice what was going on: how I was feeling, the tone of my thoughts, my energy levels, and my physical state. They also become a place to acknowledge myself for things no one else saw: "That was a tough conversation, I'm proud of you for staying open." "You weren't feeling well today and you still showed up with grace."

These weren't achievement lists or failure lists, they were acknowledgments of the messy business of living.

Years later, when I decided to share some of these notes on social media, people responded with "Wow, relationship goals!" and "What an amazing partner," thinking the handwritten messages were from my significant other. I beamed with pride knowing these notes were written to me by *me*. I had gone from that sad failure list to being relationship goals with myself.

We often worry that being kind to ourselves will make us soft, complacent, or unmotivated. But Dr. Kristin Neff's research demonstrates that self-compassionate people are more likely to take on challenges and try again after failure. In one study, participants who scored higher on self-compassion measures were more willing to receive feedback about their weaknesses and more motivated to improve themselves (Neff 2023).

Self-criticism freezes us with shame, while self-compassion gives us the emotional safety to take risks, experiment, and grow from inevitable setbacks.

This isn't a perfectly consistent practice. There are periods when my notes pile up daily, and other stretches—sometimes weeks—where I write nothing at all. Sometimes, I genuinely don't know what to write. But when I'm feeling low, anxious, or stuck, I start simply: "Sweet pea, today you are feeling [whatever emotion is present]" and let the words flow from there.

Feeding self-compassion didn't starve my inner critic to death. That harsh voice still pipes up, especially when I'm tired or stressed. But now I recognize it for what it is—a misguided attempt to protect me—and I can (sometimes) gently redirect it. "Thanks for trying to keep me safe," I tell it, "but I've got this."

Writing love notes might feel too earnest (my own inner critic thinks it's kind of cringe), so know that self-compassion comes in many forms. Try simply placing a hand on your heart when you are struggling or creating an alter ego to give you pep talks in a funny voice. Some people prefer to have a single phrase like "This is hard, and that's ok." The form matters less than the intention: skipping the failure list and instead giving yourself the kindness you'd offer a friend.

PLAY YOUR HEART OUT

Think about it this way: If you were on a track team and showed up one day depleted from lack of sleep, what would motivate you better? A coach who screamed "You suck! Why are you so slow today?! Keep running until you get faster!" or a coach who said "I know you have greatness in you, I've seen it. Today, you're running slower than usual... maybe you need to rest and come back strong tomorrow"? Which of these coaches would you be enthused to run for the next day?

If you'd choose the kind coach, research is on your side. In her book *The Willpower Instinct*, psychologist Kelly McGonigal references studies that show an interesting pattern: Students who responded to procrastination with harsh self-criticism procrastinated even more on future exams. Meanwhile, the ones who practiced self-forgiveness were able to break the pattern of procrastination on future tests (McGonigal 2013). The research shows how beating yourself up makes you more likely to repeat the same mistake. Self-compassion, not self-punishment, helps us move forward and do better next time.

Forgiveness, not guilt. Compassion, not criticism. Here's the magic of self-compassion: It doesn't diminish your appetite for achievement. Instead, it gives you the energy to play, to create, to stick your neck out in ways that your inner critic never would have allowed.

Lauren Phaneuf dreamed of roller skating as a child but wasn't allowed to pursue it. As an adult, her negative self-chatter was loud: "You're too old to start roller skating." "Don't embarrass yourself."

Then, at age forty, Lauren and a friend had this bold idea to start a roller club, even without any experience. With the support of her friend, she began taking lessons. At first, she was still self-conscious and her self-talk was abrasive. But as she put more effort toward compassionately coaching herself, her confidence grew. She kept a skate diary where she made notes about what she was learning and her goals, and gave little pep talks to herself.

For the first few years, she wouldn't dare film herself, but as she started to grow within her mind, she became more comfortable with vulnerability. She even started a TikTok of her skating—not for followers or views, but to see her own progress and celebrate how far she'd come.

Powered by this progress, her courage bloomed into new dimensions. She wrote a poem about skating and read it at an arts festival in front of a crowd—something she'd been scared to do her whole life.

Now she shares her challenges and wins vulnerably, connecting with others and helping them skate toward self-kindness too.

When we stop making mental inventories of all the ways we're failing, we use our energy more productively to channel our supportive coach, who brings orange slices for after the game and makes sure you're hydrated before you get out there and play again.

CRYING INTO CONFETTI

Sometimes, allowing ourselves to play can open us up to emotions we've been avoiding. And that's when we need self-compassion the most.

I didn't expect to cry into the confetti. But I understand why I did.

I had signed up to attend the Confetti Project, a celebratory play experience. But when the day of the event came, I wasn't in a merry mood at all. As I rode the subway there, my thoughts were a punishing loop, tears threatened to spill, and I seriously wanted to disappear myself.

But I'd committed to going, so I willed myself to show up.

The room was a color explosion with rainbow confetti gathered in piles. We were invited to explore. I tentatively touched the tissue paper pieces, listened to them crinkle, lifted a handful in the air, and then watched them drift down like petals in the breeze. In my shaky state, it was scary to drop my defenses enough to play, even in this small way.

The experience unfolded gently. We talked with new people, danced in a circle together, and repeatedly threw confetti in the air. Despite feeling heavy, I found myself caught up in a state of wonder as I watched other people's faces light up like children, as confetti rained down around them.

Then came the final moment: "Lie down and close your eyes."

I settled onto the rainbow-dotted floor, tissue paper rumpling under me, colorful pieces tangled in my hair. The room grew quiet.

But the instant I lay down, something cracked open and tears started streaming down my face. Chest-heaving sobs came from somewhere deep inside of me. I wasn't crying from joy. I was crying from a truth I'd been hiding from for weeks: I was depressed. Lying there in the midst of celebration, I finally admitted it to myself.

Play requires so much more vulnerability than we realize. To play in earnest, we have to let our guard down and open ourselves up—which also risks exposing the emotions that we've been stuffing behind closed doors. Playing unlocks all the good stuff in life: the vibrancy, connection, and ecstasy of existence. It can also unearth pain. To live fully, we have to accept it all.

Without self-compassion, we might interpret these moments of emotional release as proof that we shouldn't play or open up. But with self-compassion, we can recognize these moments as invitations to heal and live more authentically.

When we all sat up again, the room was a blurred kaleidoscope through my wet eyes. The woman next to me reached out across and squeezed my hand in recognition. Though I felt a bit ridiculous blubbering in a room full of strangers, what I felt most was relief. The play had created space for me to acknowledge what I had been carrying.

Giving yourself permission to play is an act of bravery that will lead you to a fully lived life. A life worth celebrating.

Even if the confetti gets a bit tear-stained along the way.

You Feed Yourself Love When You:

- Treat your needs like VIPs (very important priorities);
- Welcome your feelings (even the uncomfy ones);
- Make space for your desires;
- Let yourself be weirdly, wonderfully imperfect;
- Talk to yourself like a bestie would;
- Thank your past self (they gave their all);

- Keep your future self in mind;
- Forgive your mistakes, no matter how messy;
- Clap for your triumphs, big and small;
- Give yourself permission to play.

THE CUPID OF CRINGE

Courage starts with showing up and letting ourselves be seen.

Brené Brown

"WHAT WAS I THINKING?" I stared at my reflection in the mirror, a riot of pink and red staring back at me. The bubblegum-pink A-line dress, the fuchsia tights, the heart-shaped glasses, and to top it all off, a red cowboy hat.

It was Valentine's Day 2021 and for some reason I could no longer recall, I had decided I would dress as Cupid and go pass out love notes to strangers on the New York City subway. Had I lost a bet? No. You know me well enough by now to know that this was entirely my own idea.

The pandemic was winding down, people were isolated, and I hatched this grand plan to create a "love mob" with friends. But surprisingly, "Hey, want to dress up like a Valentine's Day explosion and accost pandemic-weary New Yorkers on the subway?" wasn't the compelling invitation I thought it would be. Suddenly everyone was very busy and all but one declined.

Most people might take this as a sign to call it quits. Not I!

I wasn't totally alone in my mission. My friend Sophia, bless her, had agreed to come along. Not to participate, per se. Rather, she'd volunteered to document this adventure.

So there I was, carrying a bag of violet handmade zines, several heart-painted signs, and a bag of lollipops.

With a deep breath, I headed into the subway, Sophia trailing behind me like a cheerful documentary filmmaker.

As we descended the subway steps, my brain bully started up: "Ew, this is so earnest! Why do you have to be like this?" But another voice, the one that loves adventure and believes in spreading joy, pushed me on: "Let's do this," it said. "New York needs a little love. And besides, in this city you really can never be too weird."

I put on my pastel-pink N95 mask and began approaching strangers. "I made this for you," I told a group of teenagers, hesitantly. They glanced at the zines, exchanged looks, and walked away without taking them. A flush crept up my cheeks, but Sophia's presence pushed me forward.

As I continued on my mission, playing "Groove Is in the Heart" on my little portable speaker, several people acted like I was invisible and I wished I could disappear. A businessman in a sharp suit gave me a look of deep disdain. A group of friends chuckled as I passed. People veered away from me dramatically as though I were wielding a weapon, not a "Tap for a Love Boost" sign.

I found an empty bench and sat down, taking a moment to regroup. My inner critic was having a field day. "This is humiliating," it sneered. I considered bailing on the whole thing.

As we sat there, I started to notice the vibrant tapestry of New York life around us. An exuberant character wearing rainbow-colored everything that made my outfit look positively understated. Dancers yelling, "Showtime!" and defying gravity as they swirled around the subway pole. A caped performer dancing jauntily while playing the flute.

I watched as people brushed by them briskly, some actively swerving to avoid them. I empathized with these performers, wowed by their fortitude to keep playing. As I showed myself some kindness, accepting my own awkwardness and persistence, I surged with compassion for them too.

"You know what?" I said to Sophia. "This is my way of giving back to New York. By being one of its blessed weirdos that add texture and life to the city."

With renewed determination and a softer heart, I picked up my signs and started again. This time, when people brushed me off, I didn't let it dampen my spirit. I focused on the few who smiled, the occasional person who accepted a zine with interest, the kinship with every street performer and clipboard-wielding charity worker I passed.

Then, unexpectedly, a very cool group of twenty-somethings who I thought would ignore me cheered and high-fived me. Then a teenager asked me for a hug. As I continued, I found more moments like this—a young person who teared up at the gesture, a couple who asked for extra zines to share with friends, a businesswoman who said my outfit brightened her day.

As we closed out our Valentine's Day adventure in Union Square, where street performers, artists, and everyday New Yorkers created a swirling soup of urban life, I caught sight of a group of breakdancers in identical jumpsuits. One of them smiled at my outrageous outfit, and I smiled back, offering a lollipop and a zine.

"How do you keep going when reactions are mixed?" I asked.

"It's all part of the gig," they said. "Some days are brutal, some are great. I keep showing up. Plus, you never really know who you might inspire or connect with."

As I watched them flip and spin, cheered on by the small but appreciative crowd, I realized that this is what it means to live playfully. It's not about being the most talented or the most outgoing. It's about being brave enough to try.

Play is an act of courage. It's committing to our dreams and desires, no matter how out-there they are. (Like, say, deciding to play New York City subway Cupid.) It's about daring to be vulnerable in pursuit of connection and joy.

I looked down at my zine, rereading the rhyme I'd written:

> Hey, it's Hearts Day
> Let's spread love
> Smile at strangers
> Give a hug
> Know that love has many forms
> Not just romantic (Break those norms!)
> Share admiration, say oooh and ahhh
> Cheer your people, say hoorah
> And for yourself, most tenderness
> We're all full of love and all a mess

These words weren't just for Valentine's Day. They were a rhyming rallying cry for every day.

As the dancers finished, I joined in the applause, with a surge of affection for my city and all the brave players in it.

We're all buskers in our own way. Whether we're performing on a stage, pitching an idea in a boardroom, or simply saying hello to a stranger, we're all putting ourselves out there, hoping to connect.

The more we can approach ourselves and each other with compassion, the safer it becomes to play, to take risks, to be our authentic selves.

So here's to the buskers, the dreamers, the love-note writers, and everyone brave enough to show up. The world is more vivid and alive because of you. May we be kind to ourselves when we stumble and always, always, always keep playing.

* * *

Throughout this book, we've explored the many facets of playful living. Self-compassion is the nourishing soil that allows courage to flourish and lets us step into the unknown and dare to dream.

The practices in this book aren't meant to be approached with rigid discipline. They're invitations to cultivate a devoted relationship with your playful self. Some days, you might fully embrace wonder-finding or build elaborate play dates. Other days, your playful devotion might look like forgiving yourself for being too exhausted to do anything but rest. It all counts. Every tiny step matters, especially the ones that are hardest to take.

Your "Don't Eat Yourself Alive!" Toolkit
Develop Your Powers of Self-Compassion

The Flash Recap: Self-compassion doesn't diminish your drive for growth—it provides the resilience and courage needed to play bigger and bolder. When you replace harsh self-criticism with gentle encouragement, you free up vast reserves of energy for creativity, connection, and joy.

Wiggle Room: When your internal judge pipes up today, pause, place a hand on your heart, and tell yourself, "This is human." Micro-moments of compassion add up.

Play Practice
"So, How'd It Go?" Reflection

A compassionate look back after taking risks

When you put yourself out there or take risks, your inner critic often hijacks the post-game commentary. This practice gives you a kinder framework for processing what happened. As you try new things from this book, use this to assess more generously.

What did you try? Briefly describe the experience or give it a headline.

3 Things That Went Well: Note your successes, no matter how small.

3 Things You Can Celebrate Yourself For: Practice explicit self-appreciation; commend your bravery.

2 Things You Learned: Focus on growth and insights.

2 Things You Want to Do Differently Next Time: Look forward constructively.

1 EEK! You DON'T Want to Do Again: Learn from difficulties without dwelling on them. Laugh if you can.

You'll strengthen your ability to take risks with this practice, knowing you'll process the experience with compassion rather than criticism. The goal isn't to grade yourself, but to gather insights while treating yourself like a good friend would.

CONCLUSION

The World Awaits Your Playful Spirit

Now that you're almost at the very end of the book, I am going to let you in on my ulterior motive for inviting you here (yes, an ulterior motive—how sneaky!). My hope is that when you close this book—poof!—you will become an envoy of play. As an agent of the Playful Way you will be a critical puzzle piece in assembling a more playful world.

In the reality that you'll help create, playfulness is not something to be tucked away for a rainy day; it's a core practice building new realities in our homes, our offices, our schools, and our institutions—filling them with the tinkering sounds of experimentation, the diffusing roars of laughter, and the wide-eyed wonder of renewing our wows.

This is a place where we're allowed to shape-shift and change, to make mistakes. It's a place where compassion flows, where self-kindness is the air we fill our lungs with, and where the courage to be vulnerable grows like cheerful wildflowers in a summer field.

This way of approaching our day-to-day lives imbues them with more curiosity, creativity, and connectedness.

A playful world is a better-resourced world. It's a place adept at improvising with change. One where we are equipped to handle challenges and dream up new ways of existing.

Where a treasure trove of funny memories, inside jokes, and

bonding experiences tethers us to each other. A world full of collaboration and empathy, where we are bonded by the flexible glue of play.

CELEBRATING YOUR PLAYFUL JOURNEY

Look how far you've come! Through these pages, you've built invaluable skills. You've discovered that play isn't frivolous—it's fundamental to a rich, resilient life.

You've learned to unzip your Serious Suit, letting your inner Joyful Jester emerge with all its unguarded, humorous spirit. You've practiced looking for pink flamingos, training your Visionary Dreamer to see possibilities where others see limitations.

You've embraced the "Yes, and" approach of your Adventurous Improviser, building flexibility muscles that will serve you through life's unexpected plot twists. Your Expressive Creator has discovered how to create meaning even in difficult experiences through artistic exploration. Your Mundane Alchemist has figured out how to make routine chores into a flight of whimsy.

You've learned to embrace your Mover & Shaker and get out of your head, letting your body lead you to solutions your mind alone couldn't reach. Your Wonder Wanderer has awakened, noticing the extraordinary hiding in plain sight.

Your Curious Quester has remembered that experimentation isn't about winning or losing; it's about learning and growing. And perhaps most important, you've practiced self-compassion, treating yourself with the kindness that builds courage.

Will the Playful Way always be easy? Of course not. Life will still life, days will be full of obstacles, the tough times won't go away. But now you know that play isn't the opposite of seriousness—it's the thing that makes seriousness bearable. It's the lantern that lights your way through the gloom, the laughter that shakes off stress, the gentle landing when you inevitably fall.

Every time you embrace your playful nature, you give others permission to do the same. You become a beacon of joy, a catalyst for creativity.

Can you feel it? The lightness in your step, the twinkle in your eye, the bounce in your heart? This power of play is waiting for you (for all of us!) to embrace it.

I'm getting down on one knee now and offering you a heart-shaped mood ring. Will you be an envoy of the playful spirit? Will you give yourself permission to play in small and big moments? Will you play in sickness and in health? Will you look at the world in wonder with a sense of sparkling possibility?

The world needs your unique brand of playfulness. I hope you'll say I DO!

[CUE MUSIC & INSERT CONFETTI DROP HERE]

ON PLAY RIPPLES

Before you go, a story that started it all . . .

In the summer of 2022, I stood at a crossroads. For years, I had witnessed the transformative power of play in my work as a creative leader, a teacher, and a mother. I'd seen how playfulness could help people process emotions, spark brilliant ideas, and come alive like nothing else could. A quiet voice inside me kept suggesting that I should dedicate my next career chapter to bringing more play into people's lives.

But doubt crept in. Could I really build a career around something as misunderstood as play in adulthood? Would people truly see a need for this in our achievement-obsessed world? The questions swirled, leaving me stuck between possibility and practicality.

"Why don't you ask the universe for a sign?" my friend Sophia suggested.

"Why not?" I thought. And so I did. On a gray July day, while visiting my in-laws in Cologne, Germany, I set out on a long walk along the Rhine River in search of a sign. The heavy clouds matched my uncertain mood. I passed a street carnival in the midst of being set up, its colors dulled by the overcast sky. Not my sign. I kept walking. I came across a playground with an imposing metal slide that resembled a medieval torture device. Not my sign either, I decided.

As I considered turning to head back, the sun began to break through the clouds. I made my way down to the river's edge to take in the view of the Cologne Cathedral across the water. And then I heard it—a gentle clinking sound at my feet.

There, knocking against the pebbled shore, was a textured glass bottle with a rolled up piece of paper inside.

Gasps A message in a bottle.

With heart fluttering from excitement and disbelief, I retrieved it from the water. Inside was a letter complete with a crimson wax seal. On paper with wavy, burnt edges, a seven-year-old named Eliano wrote about his love for art, nature, and play ("spielen" because it was written in German).

If this wasn't the sign I was looking for, I don't know what would be.

After writing to the address included in the bottle, I learned the message was part of a creative project that Eliano had done with his mother, Kristina, during the pandemic. Launching their bottled message into the Rhine was just one of fifty activities to bring joy and connection into a time of isolation.

As we continued to correspond, they sent photographs of their bucket list adventures—campfires, stargazing, homegrown gardens, and museum visits. Eventually, a handmade scrapbook arrived in my mailbox, filled with quotes and stickers about creativity and play.

The World Awaits Your Playful Spirit

This story still stuns me. A family using play to find joy and connection in uncertainty inadvertently encouraged me to help others do the same. Their bottle, launched with hope but no expectations, traveled for months before delivering its message precisely where it needed to go.

I often think about what would have happened if I hadn't gone down to the river's edge at that exact moment. What if I hadn't heard the clinking of glass against stone? What if I'd dismissed it as litter rather than treasure?

But here's the thing . . . when we approach life with playful curiosity, we create space for magic to enter. We notice the clinking bottles at our feet. We pull on threads of curiosity. We follow signs. We make huge life decisions guided by serendipity.

And sometimes, like Eliano's family, we create ripples of playfulness that travel farther than we could ever imagine, touching lives we'll never know about in ways we couldn't predict.

Nearly a year after finding that bottle, I followed the sign and launched a play company, and shortly after that, I started working on this book. I still have doubts some days—who doesn't? But then I remember that unlikely messenger, that bottle that traveled a river to find me, and I keep going.

The universe had answered my question about whether to focus on play with the perfect response. A message I am now passing along to you:

Play on. The ripples you create might just be someone else's sign.

ACKNOWLEDGMENTS

Heartfelt thanks to my agent Cindy Uh for waiting years for me to be ready to write a book, for fiercely advocating for me, and for being so encouraging in her directness that I took "Start over with a blank page" as loving feedback, not crushing defeat. To Gabriella Page-Fort, my delightful editor, who took this project on with curiosity and openness, road testing these ideas in her own life and pushing this book to be ever more expansive. I had so much fun working with you—wind in our hair is always a good thing! Ryan Amato, thank you for keeping our i's dotted, our t's crossed, and the play train running on time—choo choo!

Anna Pastenbach, thank you for bringing me into the HarperOne family and seeing the potential in *The Playful Way*.

I would have been adrift at sea without the anchoring presence of Sam Amberg, my creative copilot, who was with me since the first seeds of the book started growing in my mind and we sat together in the sunshine scribbling out the first proposal outline. A constant thought partner, believer, and first reader, Sam's artistic approach to life (and neuroscience knowledge) blessed so many corners of this project. And to Sam's dad, Mark Louis Amberg, who died while we were working on this book: Your joyful, spontaneous, creative spirit lives on in these pages. You've certainly made your Mark.

Everlasting appreciation to my writing group chat, Liz Tran and Lydia Pang—my absolute *angels*, whose camaraderie, vulnerability, and insights carried me through this process. All the hours of voice notes back and forth, writing "route talk," and rallying were an absolute lifeline in what would have otherwise been a crushingly lonely process. I'd walk a thousand miles for a ham sandwich with you (says the vegetarian).

Adoration for my courageous, audacious, and extra-vivacious daughter, Viva, who has taught me so much about what it means to live playfully.

Special love to my partner, Philippe, for dancing with my silly spirit all these years, knowing when my soul desperately needs a rave, and for nudging me to take the space I needed to get this project done.

Of course I'd never be here without my family, my original play crew. Thank you to Mom for reading to us nightly in character voices and encouraging a love of storytelling; Dad for teaching us to see the recycling bin as an art supply store; and my brother, Pepin, for being my pirate ship partner and co-architect in minigolf course construction, and for giving me a level of humor to ever aspire to. To my sister Teresa for always getting the dance party going and giving life to my greatest dream.

This book was enriched by everyone I interviewed; whether I included your words directly or not, your influence lives in these pages. Dr. Joanna Fortune, Sarah Gough at Play for Peace, Michelle Lee, Suleika Jaouad, Oliver Jeffers, Roya Partovi, Babba Rivera, Mayssa Chehata, Marissa Hamamoto, Sophia Li, Dan Saks, Anjelika Temple, Liz Tran, Dev Aujla, Lydia Pang, Nadya Okamoto, Kate Thompson, Camilla Pang, Jose Duyanda, Tania Kottoor, Daisy Auger-Domínguez, Susan McPherson, Sam Furness, Linda Marie Armstrong, Carina Sherman, Sam Reece, Brendan Boyle, and everyone else my tired writer's brain is forgetting—thank you for sharing your wisdom.

A special nod to the teachers who cheered and challenged me to push my creative bounds over the years, including Ms. Miller, Ms. White, Lee Dejasu, Nancy Barton, Keith Mayerson, Adam Wade, Georgia Clark, Casey Erin Clark, Julie Fogh, and Debbie Attias.

Acknowledgments

I've been lifted by my many friends who encouraged and inspired this work: Aziz Hasan, Rebecca Friedman, Maria Jia Ling Pitt, Madison Utendahl, Nikkia Reveillac, Roanne Adams, Morgan First, Lakshmi Narayanee, Belen Tenorio and Cherri Hartigan (my Magic League), and my 2021 Artist's Way group.

The physical spaces where I wrote deserve their own acknowledgment: the Brass Factory in Brooklyn, which tolerated my silly dance breaks as I pieced my proposal together; The Hummingbird in LA, where many of the rhyming poems were written, and its generous hosts, the Adams-Wahba family; the cozy and artistic Woodstock Way Hotel in Woodstock, New York, where I holed up with Liz to write in the snow; and Sound View on the North Fork of Long Island, where I was reminded of my beachcomber's eye while wandering the pebbly shore.

The universe works in mysterious ways—thank you to the Mirabella family for sending that message in a bottle that became a sign to write this book.

Finally, my heart forever is grateful to all the creative spirits who've collaborated and joined me in my myriad creative pursuits over the years—your energy and imagination continue to remind me why play matters so much. To past Piera for all her TLC on this project. I'm excited to see where this takes us and for the version of you that comes next.

And to you, dear reader, thanks for playing. <3

BIBLIOGRAPHY

Agarwal, Pragya. "Understanding Unconscious Bias." Interview by Emily Kwong. *Short Wave*, NPR. July 15, 2020. https://www.npr.org/2020/07/14/891140598/understanding-unconscious-bias

Andrade, Jackie. "What Does Doodling Do?" *Applied Cognitive Psychology* 24, no. 1 (2009): 100–106. https://doi.org/10.1002/acp.1561.

Berk, L. S., et al. Modulation of neuroimmune parameters during the eustress of humor-associated mirthful laughter. *Alternative Therapies in Health and Medicine* 7, no. 2 (2001): 62–76.

Bernardi, Nicolò F., Matteo De Buglio, Pietro D. Trimarchi, Alfonso Chielli, and Emanuela Bricolo. "Mental Practice Promotes Motor Anticipation: Evidence from Skilled Music Performance." *Frontiers in Human Neuroscience* 7 (2013). https://doi.org/10.3389/fnhum.2013.00451.

Breines, Juliana G., and Serena Chen. "Self-Compassion Increases Self-Improvement Motivation." *Personality and Social Psychology Bulletin* 38, no. 9 (2012): 1133–43. https://doi.org/10.1177/0146167212445599.

Brown, Stuart L. "Consequences of Play Deprivation." Scholarpedia, April 19, 2013. http://dx.doi.org/10.4249/scholarpedia.30449.

Deterding, Sebastian, Dan Dixon, Rilla Khaled, and Lennart Nacke. "From Game Design Elements to Gamefulness." *Proceedings of the 15th International Academic MindTrek Conference: Envisioning Future Media Environments*, 2011, 9–15. https://doi.org/10.1145/2181037.2181040.

Gelardi, Piera. "What Actually Got Me Through My Miscarriage." Refinery29, September 14, 2017.

Gocłowska, Małgorzata A., Simone M. Ritter, Andrew J. Elliot, and Matthijs Baas. "Novelty Seeking Is Linked to Openness and Extraversion, and Can Lead to Greater Creative Performance." *Journal of Personality* 87, no. 2 (2018): 252–66. https://doi.org/10.1111/jopy.12387.

Hayes, Steven C., Jason B. Luoma, Frank W. Bond, Akihiko Masuda, and Jason Lillis. "Acceptance and Commitment Therapy: Model, Processes and Outcomes." *Behaviour Research and Therapy* 44, no. 1 (2006): 1–25.

Hmelo-Silver, Cindy E. "Problem-Based Learning: What and How Do Students Learn?" *Educational Psychology Review* 16, no. 3 (2004): 235–66. https://doi.org/10.1023/b:edpr.0000034022.16470.f3.

Kashdan, Todd B., and Jonathan Rottenberg. "Psychological Flexibility as a Fundamental Aspect of Health." *Clinical Psychology Review* 30, no. 7 (2010): 865–78.

Kramer, Caroline Kaercher, and Cristiane Bauermann Leitao. "Laughter as Medicine: A Systematic Review and Meta-Analysis of Interventional Studies Evaluating the Impact of Spontaneous Laughter on Cortisol Levels." *PLOS One* 18, no. 5 (2023). https://doi.org/10.1371/journal.pone.0286260.

Lebuda, Izabela, Darya L. Zabelina, and Maciej Karwowski. "Mind Full of Ideas: A Meta-Analysis of the Mindfulness–Creativity Link." *Personality and Individual Differences* 93 (2016): 22–26. https://doi.org/10.1016/j.paid.2015.09.040.

Le Cunff, Anne-Laure. *Tiny Experiments: How to Live Freely in a Goal-Obsessed World*. New York: Avery, 2025.

Lee, Sarah, Jared B. Kenworthy, and Paul B. Paulus. "Effects of Positive Affect and Humor on Divergent Thinking." *Journal of Creativity* 32, no. 3 (2022): article 100037. https://doi.org/10.1016/j.yjoc.2022.100037.

Lieberoth, Andreas. "Shallow Gamification." *Games and Culture* 10, no. 3 (2014): 229–48. https://doi.org/10.1177/1555412014559978.

Martin, Rod, and Nicholas A. Kuiper. "Three Decades Investigating Humor and Laughter: An Interview with Professor Rod Martin." *Europe's Journal of Psychology* 12, no. 3 (2016): 498–512. https://doi.org/10.5964/ejop.v12i3.1119.

McBride, Hillary L. *The Wisdom of Your Body: Finding Healing, Wholeness, and Connection Through Embodied Living*. Ada, MI: Brazos Press, 2001.

McGonigal, Kelly. *The Willpower Instinct: How Self-Control Works, Why It Matters, and What You Can Do to Get More of It*. New York: Avery, 2013.

Meister, I. G, T. Krings, H. Foltys, B. Boroojerdi, M. Müller, R. Töpper, and A. Thron. "Playing Piano in the Mind—an fMRI Study on Music Imagery and Performance in Pianists." *Cognitive Brain Research* 19, no. 3 (2004): 219–28. https://doi.org/10.1016/j.cogbrainres.2003.12.005.

Miller, Chanel. "92. Chanel Miller Promises: We are Never Stuck." Interview by Glennon Doyle, Abby Wambach, and Amanda Doyle. *We Can Do Hard Things*. Podcast audio. May 3, 2022. https://podcasts.apple.com/us/podcast/92-chanel-miller-promises-we-are-never-stuck/id1564530722?i=1000559421614.

Neff, Kristin. "Being Kind to Yourself." Interview by Shankar Vendantam. *Hidden Brain*. Podcast audio. September 3, 2023. https://hiddenbrain.org/podcast/being-kind-to-yourself/.

Oppezzo, Marily, and Daniel L. Schwartz. "Give Your Ideas Some Legs: The Positive Effect of Walking on Creative Thinking." *Journal of Experimental Psychology: Learning, Memory, and Cognition* 40, no. 4 (2014): 1142–52. https://doi.org/10.1037/a0036577.

Park, Guihyun, Beng-Chong Lim, and Hui Si Oh. "Why Being Bored Might Not Be a Bad Thing After All." *Academy of Management Discoveries* 5, no. 1 (2019): 78–92. https://doi.org/10.5465/amd.2017.0033.

Pearson, D. G. "Mental Imagery and Creative Cognition." In *The Routledge International Handbook of Creative Cognition*, edited by Linden J. Ball and Frédéric Vallée-Tourangeau. London: Routledge, 2023.

Proyer, René T. "The Well-Being of Playful Adults: Adult Playfulness, Subjective Well-Being, Physical Well-Being, and the Pursuit of Enjoyable Activities." *European Journal of Humour Research* 1, no. 1 (2013): 84–98. https://doi.org/10.7592/ejhr2013.1.1.proyer.

Reddan, Marianne Cumella, Tor Dessart Wager, and Daniela Schiller. "Attenuating Neural Threat Expression with Imagination." *Neuron* 100, no. 4 (2018). https://doi.org/10.1016/j.neuron.2018.10.047.

Reynolds, Gretchen. "How Exercise May Help the Brain Grow Stronger." *New York Times*, June 15, 2016. https://nyti.ms/3BvQQRY.

Stuckey, Heather L., and Jeremy Nobel. "The Connection Between Art, Healing, and Public Health: A Review of Current Literature." *American Journal of Public Health* 100, no. 2 (2010): 254–63. https://doi.org/10.2105/ajph.2008.156497.

Walker, Sarah A., Rebecca T. Pinkus, Sally Olderbak, and Carolyn MacCann. "People with Higher Relationship Satisfaction Use More Humor, Valuing, and Receptive Listening to Regulate Their Partners' Emotions." *Current Psychology* 43, no. 3 (2023): 2348–56. https://doi.org/10.1007/s12144-023-04432-4.

Zanto, Theodore P., and Adam Gazzaley. "Aging of the Frontal Lobe." *Handbook of Clinical Neurology* 163 (2019): 369–89. https://doi.org/10.1016/b978-0-12-804281-6.00020-3.

Ziv, Avner. "Facilitating Effects of Humor on Creativity." *Journal of Educational Psychology* 68, no. 3 (1976): 318–22. https://doi.org/10.1037/0022-0663.68.3.318.

Sources and References

Brown, Stuart. *Play: How It Shapes the Brain, Opens the Imagination, and Invigorates the Soul.* New York: Avery, 2009.

Fortune, Joanna. *Why We Play: How to Find Joy and Meaning in Everyday Life.* London: Vermilion, 2022.

Kashdan, Todd B., and Jonathan Rottenberg. "Psychological Flexibility as a Fundamental Aspect of Health." *Clinical Psychology Review* 30, no. 7 (2010): 865–78.

Kent, Corita, and Jan Steward. *Learning by Heart: Teachings to Free the Creative Spirit.* 2nd ed. New York: Allworth Press, 2008.

McGonigal, Kelly. *The Joy of Movement: How Exercise Helps Us Find Happiness, Hope, Connection, and Courage.* New York: Avery, 2019.

Pethick, Paul. *The Power of Play: How Play and Its Games Shape Our Lives.* Self-published, 2019.

Further Reading and Resources

Cameron, Julia. *The Artist's Way: A Spiritual Path to Higher Creativity.* 25th anniversary ed. New York: TarcherPerigee, 2016.

Carse, James P. *Finite and Infinite Games: A Vision of Life as Play and Possibility.* New York: Free Press, 1986.

Creative Mornings. https://creativemornings.com.

Gilbert, Elizabeth. *Big Magic: Creative Living Beyond Fear.* New York: Riverhead Books, 2015.

Jaouad, Suleika. *The Book of Alchemy: A Creative Practice for An Inspired Life.* New York: Penguin Random House, 2025.

Keltner, Dacher. *Awe: The New Science of Everyday Wonder and How It Can Transform Your Life.* New York: Penguin Press, 2023.

NoomaLooma. https://noomalooma.com.

Resnick, Mitchel. *Lifelong Kindergarten: Cultivating Creativity Through Projects, Passion, Peers, and Play.* Cambridge: MIT Press, 2017.

Smith, Keri. *How to Be an Explorer of the World: Portable Life Museum.* New York: Penguin Books, 2008.

Ter Kuile, Casper. *The Power of Ritual: Turning Everyday Activities into Soulful Practices.* New York: HarperOne, 2020.

Zevin, Gabrielle. *Tomorrow, and Tomorrow, and Tomorrow.* New York: Knopf, 2022.

ABOUT THE AUTHOR

Piera Gelardi is a creative entrepreneur, speaker, and artist passionate about bringing play into every room she enters. She cofounded the influential media brand Refinery29 and its magical pop-up, 29Rooms, earning recognition as one of *Ad Age*'s "50 Most Creative People" and *Entrepreneur*'s "50 Most Daring Entrepreneurs." Through her new company, NoomaLooma, and her energetic keynotes, Piera helps people unlock their creative superpowers. When she's not playing professionally, she loves hosting noodle and doodle nights, throwing spontaneous dance parties, and making up songs with her daughter, Viva.

Follow her at @PieraLuisa on Instagram and Substack, or visit www.pieragelardi.com.